Pasta Pronto!

Pasta

Pronto!

The Ultimate Guide
to Creating Delicious Dishes
with Your Pasta Machine

Lisë Stern

HPBooks

HPBooks
Published by The Berkley Publishing Group
A member of Penguin Putnam Inc.
200 Madison Avenue
New York, NY 10016

Copyright © 1997 by Lisë Stern
Book design by Richard Oriolo
Cover design and illustration by Charles Björklund

First edition: November 1997

Published simultaneously in Canada.

The Putnam Berkley World Wide Web site address is
http://www.berkley.com

Library of Congress Cataloging-in-Publication Data

Stern, Lisë.
    Pasta Pronto! :   the ultimate guide to creating delicious
dishes with your pasta machine / Lisë Stern. — 1st ed.
        p.   cm.
    Includes index.
    ISBN 1-55788-276-2
    1. Cookery (Pasta) 2. Pasta machines. I. Title.
TX809.M17S74   1997   97-9778
641.8'72—dc21   CIP

Printed in the United States of America

10   9   8   7   6   5   4   3   2   1

To my family,
Jeffrey, Gabriel, Eitan, and Shoshanna,
with love

Contents

Acknowledgments

A number of people helped make this book a possibility.

Special thanks to my agent, Doe Coover, for her dedication and perseverance in turning a possibility into a reality. Without her, *Pasta Pronto!* could not have been written.

Thanks to my family of pasta lovers: my husband, Jeffrey Robbins, from whom I learned much about the art of pasta and sauce making; my sons Gabriel and Eitan, who enthusiastically enjoyed using pasta machines and experimenting with different shapes and flavors ("Let's make really long orange spaghetti!"); and my daughter, Shoshanna, who helped consume these recipes in utero, and gave me an excuse to eat seconds.

For testing recipes and offering advice and opinions, thanks to Cathy Walthers, and to Kim Sundik Mayone, for her ongoing terrific spirit and support. Michele Topor and Lilly d'Alelio offered invaluable tips on pasta making, especially gnocchi.

Special thanks to my editor, Jeanette Egan, for choosing to publish this book, and for her patience and guidance. Thanks also to John Duff and the HPBooks staff for packaging the book so nicely.

And I'd like to thank the staff of Alef Bet Child Care, for watching my children so well, enabling me to write this book.

Thanks always to my parents, Joyce and Michael Stern, and to my in-laws, Donald and Esther Robbins, for their continuous love and support.

Pasta Pronto!

Introduction

When I was growing up during the 1960s in Washington, D.C., *pasta* was not a word commonly used. We had spaghetti, macaroni (and cheese), and egg noodles (the base for tuna-noodle casserole). The only sauce was tomato—with or without meatballs.

Washington did not have a sizable Italian population, and I was not exposed to the idea that there could be other shapes and sizes of pasta, as well as numerous sauces, until I went to college in New England, where I encountered all kinds of pastabilities—linguine, fettuccine, papardelle, ziti, penne, tortellini, manicotti—terms that may be familiar to most people now but were culinary wonders to me. I had never been a fan of spaghetti, and I discovered that the pasta shape really does make a difference. I like fettuccine and linguine and the bite-size penne much better than the slippery spaghetti I had known as a child, which never seemed able to hold sauce.

There are actually hundreds of official shapes of pasta in Italy. But pasta is more than an Italian dish. While the Italians certainly popularized it, and the favorite American pasta dishes are Italian-inspired, several cuisines around the world include pasta. The most notable among these cuisines are Asian: Japan is overflowing with noodle shops, and Vietnamese, Thai, and Chinese menus abound with noodle variations, from soups to stir-fries to salads. There are many European noodle dishes as well, but over the past century, and especially during the past two decades, we Americans have made pasta our own.

In 1904, a group of manufacturers met in Pittsburgh and formed the National Association of Macaroni and Noodle Manufacturers of America. Since the wheat of choice for pasta products is durum, and the association worked with durum growers to promote what for years was officially called "macaroni," the association started the first of many ad campaigns, "Eat More Macaroni." In 1919 they became the National Macaroni Manufacturers' Association. *Macaroni* continued to be the common term for pasta until the 1980s, when American interest in food in general and pasta in particular grew. While for years the three types of pasta the association had promoted had been macaroni, spaghetti, and egg noodles, now people were interested in all kinds of shapes and configurations. In 1983 the organization became the National Pasta Association, and in the past

decade there has been a pasta explosion. People like pasta because it is healthful, inexpensive, and tasty. According to National Pasta Association figures, which refer to dry pasta only, in 1995 Americans consumed almost 2.2 billion pounds of dry pasta and ordered over 1.1 billion plates of pasta in restaurants.

For years pasta was only available dry, unless you happened to live in a community with a large Italian population, where there might be pasta makers selling cut-to-order fettuccine or homemade ravioli. Nowadays, both small businesses and large manufacturers are making fresh pasta, available in the refrigerated case of most supermarkets, often in a variety of flavors.

But even so, commercially available flavors can be limiting. I liked the idea of making my own pasta and the flavoring possibilities, but I always felt intimidated; making it by hand seemed such an exacting procedure. In fact, I never made pasta until I received a pasta machine. Once I got to know my machine, all I wanted to do was experiment. I started with the basics—egg, spinach, and tomato. The egg pasta was so much richer tasting than any I had tried before, and the spinach and tomato both tasted like spinach and tomato, as opposed to being merely colored. I wanted to try everything—any flavor combination, any favorite dish, I wanted to make into pasta. I enjoyed trying the different dies, making not only flat pasta such as fettuccine, but tubular pasta such as penne and macaroni, and filled ravioli. Lasagne tastes infinitely better when made with fresh pasta. Plus, the pasta machine was actually fun to use—my kids love seeing the shapes extrude—and the results were invariably delicious. I decided to put down the results of my experimentation in this book.

Pasta Pronto! is organized into seven chapters covering a range of pasta styles. Most recipes are presented with a pasta and an accompanying sauce that can be prepared at the same time, so your pasta meal will be complete. Because the pasta cooks so quickly, I recommend waiting to cook the pasta until the accompanying sauce is almost ready. For sauces that require longer simmering or roasting, you can make the pasta while the sauce cooks.

And to demonstrate that your pasta machine can be used for every course, the "Not Just Pasta" chapter offers recipes for items such as breadsticks and delectable cookies.

Electric Pasta Machines and How They Work

Electric pasta machines extrude dough in a variety of shapes. The dry ingredients are mixed in a bowl with a paddle while you slowly add liquids. The dough is then extruded, via a corkscrew-like mechanism, through dies of various shapes. Most machines include macaroni, spaghetti, fettuccine, and lasagne.

There are two basic styles of machines. Simac makes one style, and Creative Technologies Corp., Popeil, and Maverick make the second style.

Simac
250 Halsey St.
Newark, NJ 07102
(800) 223–1898

Makes 1 1/2 pounds and comes with eight dies: lasagne, fettuccine, linguine, spaghetti, macaroni, bucato (hollow spaghetti), cookie disk, and pizza. An additional sixteen dies are available in stores or by mail. Simac was the first company to make pasta machines for the home, starting in 1980. Changes over the years have been slight, but the machine now available is sturdier than the original model. It has a powerful motor, and the dies are made of brass, some with plastic inserts.

The machine consists of a work bowl and a kneading paddle. The extruder part of the machine is located below the work bowl. When you are ready to extrude, you remove a plastic insert that separates the two areas. This enables the dough to enter the extruder, where a large corkscrew pushes it toward the die.

This is the high-end pasta machine: At this writing it cost about twice as much as the other machines. It has pluses and minuses. On the minus side, the dough mixing takes a little bit longer than it does with other machines, and dough sometimes needs to be broken up with a hard spatula—clumps of wetter dough take a while to incorporate. On the plus side, the machine is very sturdy. It is heavy, and has a powerful motor. The brass dies yield the most consistent pasta, and the machine by far makes the best, most even lasagne sheets.

Cuisinart until recently sold a machine manufactured by the same company that makes Simac's machines in Italy, and the dies are interchangeable. The Cuisinart machine could make up to 3 pounds of pasta. The company stopped carrying the machine (though some may still be available), and Simac may soon also sell a larger model.

Creative Technologies Corp. (CTC)
170 53rd St.
Brooklyn, NY 11232
(718) 492–8284

Machines made by Creative Technologies Corp., Popeil, and Maverick all have similar designs. The paddles mix the dough sideways in the work bowl, and the dough is extruded from the same space. The power switch has two positions: In one position, it mixes; in the other, it turns the paddle and the extruding corkscrew in the other direction, thereby extruding the dough. These machines all have a built-in blower that helps dry the pasta as it extrudes. This is generally a plus, except when you are extruding lasagne for ravioli making, and you don't want it to dry out. In such cases, gently hold the ends of the lasagne above the blower as it extrudes.

CTC makes three models of machine. All make 1 1/2 pounds of pasta. They are essentially the same design, but come with different numbers of dies:

The Creative Pasta Express X3000 comes with twelve dies: lasagne, fettuccine, linguine, spaghetti, vermicelli, small macaroni, large macaroni, rigatoni, gnocchi, bagel, breadstick, and large cookie.

The Creative Pasta Express X2000 comes with fourteen dies: lasagne, fettuccine, linguine, spaghetti, vermicelli, Oriental noodle, rotini, small macaroni, large macaroni, rigatoni, gnocchi, bagel, breadstick, and large cookie.

The Creative Pasta Express X4000 comes with eighteen dies: lasagne, fettuccine, linguine, spaghetti, vermicelli, Oriental noodle, rotini, small macaroni, large macaroni, rigatoni, gnocchi, bagel, breadstick, large cookie, tagliatelle, manicotti, shell, and pastry. It also comes with a pasta cutter and a ravioli stamp.

Popeil Pasta Products
9457 Desoto Ave.
Chatsworth, CA 91311
(800) 486–1806 or (818) 775–4680

Popeil has introduced a machine called the Popeil Pasta-Sausage Maker. If you have a Popeil Pasta Maker from before 1997, it works the same way. The company just altered the kneading paddle slightly and added sausage horns, which fit onto the machine in the same place as the pasta dies. If you like, you can buy replacement parts to adjust your machine to also do sausages. Because the product is so new, it is not entirely certain what the final packaging will be. According to a company spokesperson, it will come with three sausage horns and at least eight pasta dies, including the following: lasagne, fettuccine, linguine, spaghetti, angel hair, macaroni, rigatoni, and tagliatelle. Other kits including twelve and twenty-four dies may also be available, and you may still be able to find last year's model of the Popeil Pasta Maker.

Maverick Industries
94 Mayfield Ave.
Edison, NJ 08837
(800) 526–0954

Maverick's Pasta Del Giorno comes with eleven dies: lasagne, fettuccine, linguine, spaghetti, vermicelli (angel hair), macaroni, ziti, gnocchi, bagel, breadstick, cookie.

Pasta Ingredients

Pasta consists essentially of two kinds of ingredients: dry and liquid. The dry ingredients are grains, and the type of grain used affects how the pasta will turn out. Liquid ingredients include eggs, oil, water, juices, and fruit and vegetable purees.

Dry Ingredients

Flour The generic term *flour* refers to ground wheat. Different wheats produce different kinds of flours, with various amounts of gluten-producing protein, the element that most affects pasta. When a liquid is added to flour and the mixture is kneaded, the gluten develops. It forms elastic strands that can stretch and grow, as in bread dough, or pasta that expands when you boil it. The higher the protein, the better the pasta. Durum wheat produces a high-protein flour, and all-purpose flour is also high in protein. Cake flour is less desirable to use, as it is lower in protein.

Wheat is the only flour with a significant amount of gluten-producing protein. Flours made from other grains, such as corn, rice, or buckwheat, do not have any gluten and so must be combined with wheat flour in order to hold together well. (See the "Amber Waves of Grain" chapter for more information on various flours.)

There are two kinds of durum flour: semolina and durum. Both are pale gold in color. Semolina is coarser, and has the texture of fine cornmeal. Durum is finer, as fine as regular flour.

Commercial dry pasta is usually

made from all semolina or all durum. Semolina and durum yield a slightly denser, chewier pasta, while all-purpose flour produces a softer pasta. I experimented with various combinations, and I found that I liked a mix of equal parts of semolina and all-purpose flour. Durum works as well as semolina, but is not as readily available. I offer mail-order sources for both, as well as for other ingredients that may be hard to find. You can make very good pasta using all-purpose flour. (One of my favorites is King Arthur flour, available in supermarkets on the East Coast and also by mail, because it is unbleached and high in protein, but I like the flavor and texture semolina gives to the pasta.)

Spices and Herbs Spices and dried herbs are often added with the flour. (In some cases, fresh herbs are pureed and added with the liquids.) Any herb or spice that you like can be added to pasta—it is fun to experiment and taste the results of various combinations. Since some of the flavor is lost when the pasta is boiled, add more spice than you might otherwise if you were making something that is baked—a tablespoon versus a teaspoon, for example. The raw pasta dough may taste too strong, but the cooked product will taste just right.

Liquid Ingredients

You'll notice that most recipes give a range when they call for liquid ingredients. This is because most items that contain a large percentage of flour, such as pasta and bread, are affected by a number of factors. It may be a humid day or a dry day, so more or less liquid will be needed. The moisture content of the flour can vary, affecting how much moisture it will absorb before it reaches the proper consistency. And different liquids are absorbed more easily. For example, Basic Egg Pasta uses a greater volume of liquid than Water and Oil Pasta.

Most pasta machines come with a measuring cup with lines indicating how much flour and how much liquid to add. I recommend discarding these cups and simply following the recipes here. Those measuring cups do not give you a real sense of actual cups and tablespoons. It is easier to experiment with standard measuring cups.

Eggs Traditional fresh pasta is made with eggs, which help bind the pasta and give it flavor. Pasta made with all eggs is rich, with a somewhat chewy texture. This is a good pasta to use for ravioli, as the fat in the egg yolks makes the dough more flexible and forgiving. All the recipes in this book were made using large eggs. Some recipes use a combination of eggs and other liquids.

You may use egg whites only, or egg substitutes, which are essentially colored egg whites. Because this pasta has no oil, it is a little less flexible to work with, but the cooked results have a good texture and pleasant flavor, and the pasta has no cholesterol or fat.

Water Commercial dry pasta is made solely with semolina or durum flour and water. This is a combination that works, and the cooked results are fine, but I find many recipes work best with some fat.

Fruit and Vegetable Juices and Purees The liquid ingredients are often what give pasta its flavor. Juices such as carrot, tomato, and orange are called for. Recipes using juice usually do not contain an egg, as the egg dilutes the flavor the juice can impart to the pasta. There are some recipes calling for fruit juice concentrates, in combination with an egg, because there is more sugar in the concentrate and it needs a good binder such as an egg. I use concentrate as opposed to juice because, even when combined with the egg, it provides more flavor.

A separate category of vegetable purees comprises those used in the gnocchi chapter. Most pasta recipes have three to five times as much flour as liquid ingredient(s). Gnocchi are about 50–50 vegetable puree—namely potato, which is high in starch—to flour.

Fats Oil is the kind of fat used most often in the pasta recipes. Usually no more than 1 tablespoon of oil is used in the dough, because more than that yields a pasta that does not have a good texture.

Most recipes call for olive oil. I prefer to use extra-virgin olive oil because I like the flavor it gives dishes, but any olive oil may be used. Extra-virgin olive oil is the first pressing and has the strongest flavor. If you want a milder flavor, use virgin or pure olive oil. Most other oils may be used, with the exception of sesame oil. Even if you use only 1 tablespoon of sesame oil (any less does not really affect the flavor of the pasta), it affects the texture of the pasta, making it cook poorly. Sesame oil is fine to use in sauces, however.

Other Liquids Other liquids used include wine and other alcohol and dairy products. The alcohol in the pasta cooks out when you boil it, leaving behind a delicious flavor. I prefer using dry red or white wines mainly because I prefer drinking dry wines. But experiment with your favorites.

Several recipes, primarily for sauces, call for chicken or vegetable stock. I include recipes for these, but you can use canned, powdered, or frozen commercial stocks. Use low-sodium products, or reduce the added salt accordingly.

Milk may be used instead of water; it gives a richer taste and adds some nutritional value. Pasta made with milk will not keep as long as water-based pasta, however. Yogurt is used in some recipes, and gives the pasta a nice, tangy bite. I used nonfat yogurt. I would not recommend using something high-fat like sour cream; it can make the pasta too tender to cook properly.

Cheese

Cheese is used mostly to accompany pasta, but the Gnocchi chapter includes gnocchi made with ricotta cheese, which makes a different kind of pasta with different requirements. See the gnocchi chapter for more details. I made the recipes using both whole-milk and part-skim ricotta cheese, and both worked fine.

Many recipes call for Parmesan cheese. Unless I specify "freshly grated," I used Parmesan cheese that was already grated. But not all grated Parmesan is the same. The kind I use is in the refrigerator case. I do not recommend the cardboard containers that are miles away from any refrigeration. Imported Italian Parmesan is always the best. Freshly grated Parmesan may be used whenever regular grated Parmesan is called for in a recipe. If you have the time, it certainly tastes best.

Basic Pasta-making Techniques

Most of the recipes in this book make about 1 pound (16 ounces) of pasta—just the right amount to serve four people. Some recipes make a little more or less, and I indicate this. The pasta machines can all make up to 24 ounces of pasta. Some recipes actually serve more people, because of the accompanying ingredients.

Making pasta in an electric pasta machine does not differ significantly from machine to machine. It is important to read the instructions that come with the machine, because they indicate any specific requirements your machine may have.

If you have ever made pasta by hand, forget what you know. By hand, you knead the dough until smooth. In the machine, you want the dough to be crumbly. This is so the pieces of dough can be moved by the machine paddles into the extruder, and the extruding screw can carry them to the die. If the dough is smooth, it will be too moist for the extruder and will be sticky.

Adding Flour

First put the dry ingredients in the bowl of the machine. Run the machine for a minute to mix them. Since most recipes call for two kinds of flour, they need to mix thoroughly. In addition, this mixing helps aerate the flour, making it easier for it to absorb the liquid.

Adding Liquid

The lid of the machine has a hole or slit in it, so you can add liquids while the motor is running. This helps distribute the liquid evenly so it won't all clump up in one place. Once the flour is mixed, add the liquid ingredients while the motor is running. This should be done gradually, over 2 to 3 minutes. Generally, do not add the full amount of liquid indicated by the recipe; reserve 2 to 3 tablespoons. Since weather and other factors can affect how much liquid you need, and even 1 tablespoon can make the difference, it is best not to add it all at once. If the dough is too wet, it can be salvaged by adding more flour, but this can be tricky to do. It is easier to moisten dough that is too dry than to try to dry out wet dough. The dough should be crumbly, in clumps about the size of peas and walnuts. All the dough should be like this; if there is a lot of dough the consistency of cornmeal, it is too dry.

Mixing

After 3 minutes, check the consistency of the dough. Pinch some between your fingers and roll it. If it comes together easily and rolls without crumbling, then it is ready. If it crumbles easily and does not hold together well, it is too dry. If it holds together to the point of being almost sticky, then it is too wet.

If the dough is too dry, turn the machine back on and add additional liquid, 1/2 tablespoon at a time. Let it mix for 30 to 45 seconds before adding additional liquid. If the dough is too wet, add more semolina, 1 tablespoon at a time.

Make sure it is incorporated thoroughly before adding more. When the dough is the right consistency, it is time to extrude.

Extruding

Note that the dough that first comes out of the machine is drier and more crumbly than the dough that will follow. Usually it is a little bit of a struggle when the dough first starts to extrude, and the pasta will come out uneven and ragged. To deal with this, I recommend the following technique:

Always start with the lasagne die; this is the easiest one to clean, as it only has two large slots. Let the pasta extrude about 10 inches. Turn off the machine. Cut off this dough, tear it into smaller pieces, and return it to the machine—it will get reincorporated. Remove the lasagne die. The dough will be pressed up against it, and the edges will probably have bits of flour. Remove the dough that is right at the edge of the extrusion tube. If need be, turn on the machine and let it spin this dough out. Break this dough into a few pieces and return it to the machine. Attach the die of your choice (if you want to use the lasagne die, be sure to clean out any dough) and continue to extrude the pasta.

You also could just let the pasta extrude for 10 to 20 inches; after a minute or so, it will smooth out on its own. Return the ragged initial pasta to the work bowl.

Different dies require different attention. Tubular pasta such as macaroni and penne needs to be cut frequently. It extrudes quickly and the pieces should be 1 to 1 1/2 inches long. Make sure you have a very sharp knife for cutting the extruding pasta. Pasta such as linguine or fettuccine can extrude into longer lengths. But, as the dough extrudes, it heats up, due to the amount of friction. Use your fingers to help separate the lengths of dough so they do not stick together as they come out. Dough that is too moist in the work bowl will be stickier.

Once all the pasta has extruded, you are ready to cook or store it. The pasta can rest a little at room temperature while the water comes to a boil.

Cooking Pasta

Fresh pasta cooks much faster than dry pasta. It needs anywhere from 1 minute to 6 minutes, depending on the flour used and the size of the pasta. Angel hair pasta, the thinnest cut, cooks the fastest.

For cooking pasta you need a large stockpot that will hold at least 4 quarts of water with plenty of extra room. Stockpots are available with a metal colander insert that fits into the pot, or you can also buy such an insert separately. I highly recommend this. The insert is placed into the pot before adding the pasta. When the pasta is ready, the insert is lifted out and the hot water strained back into the pot. It is not necessary to pour the boiling water into a colander in the sink. The insert is especially useful if you are making multiple batches of pasta and you want to keep using the boiling water.

For 1 pound of pasta, bring at least 1 gallon (4 quarts) of water to a boil; I generally like to use 6 to 8 quarts. If you cover the pot with the lid, the water will come to a boil faster. Add about 1 tablespoon of salt per gallon of boiling water. The salt helps bring out the flavor of the pasta. If you need to watch your sodium intake, or if you like foods less salty, it is not necessary to salt the water.

If you do add salt to the water, wait until the water returns to a boil before adding the pasta. Add the pasta all at once (unless you are cooking it in multiple batches, as with ravioli, lasagne, and gnocchi). Stir to make sure none of the pasta sticks to the bottom of the pot. I recommend a pasta spoon—an oval, ladle-shaped spoon with dull claws around the edge for scooping and holding onto pasta, and holes in the bowl for draining out water. A pasta spoon makes it easy to retrieve a piece of pasta and test it to see if it is cooked.

Boil the pasta, uncovered, until it is *al dente*, with a small amount of firmness. If you like your pasta softer, cook it longer. The water should come back to a boil soon after you add the pasta. If the pasta has been refrigerated or frozen, the water will take a little longer to return to a boil. After 1 to 2 minutes, depending on the shape of the pasta, check the pasta for doneness. Cut a piece crosswise; it should be cooked all the way through and should not look dry in the center. Pasta that is cooked until al dente will have the barest hint of dryness but should not appear white and granular.

Drain the pasta and follow the recipe directions. If you want to serve it plain, toss it with a little olive oil to keep it from sticking and serve immediately.

Storing Pasta

Most pasta may be dried, refrigerated, or frozen. You can dry the pasta, but the point of making fresh pasta is to have it fresh. When you dry it, it loses some of its flavor and just doesn't taste as good. When refrigerated or frozen, it still maintains the taste and feel of fresh pasta. Of course, the pasta tastes best when cooked within a few hours of its being made.

To dry pasta, especially long shapes such as spaghetti or linguine, it is useful to have pasta drying racks. These are available by mail from Vitantonia and other sources (see pages 197–198). Lay the pasta over the wooden dowels and let it dry for several hours. If you are drying egg pasta, I recommend refrigerating it after it dries.

To refrigerate or freeze, let the pasta dry slightly. Dry shorter pasta on wire racks 15 to 20 minutes. This will help keep the pasta from sticking together in the refrigerator. Put the pasta in an airtight container or plastic bag and refrigerate up to 3 days or freeze up to 3 months (2 months for filled pasta). Note that refrigerated and frozen pasta takes slightly longer to cook than fresh pasta. Cook the frozen pasta directly from the freezer. Do not defrost, because the pasta will become wet and sticky.

Cleanup

As with any kind of cooking, cleaning the pasta machine is the least fun aspect of pasta making. The easiest way to clean the machine is to disassemble the various parts as soon as you are done making pasta. Set the parts on a countertop and let dry for a couple hours or overnight. The pasta dough will then easily come off. Then wash with soap and water. If you attempt to wash the bowl and dies with the pasta dough still attached, it will take much longer to clean.

Basic Recipes

The following are three basic pasta recipes. These pastas will go well with any of the sauces in the book, and will give you a sense of how to use your machine.

Basic Egg Pasta

This is the basic pasta recipe, which uses a mix of all-purpose and semolina flours and eggs—the classic pasta ingredients. It yields a rich-tasting, supple dough that is good for ravioli, when you don't want a flavored pasta to interfere with the flavors of your filling. Note that 4 eggs is slightly more than you need, and you will likely have a few tablespoons left over. Alternatively you could use 3 eggs and some water if you need extra liquid, but I prefer having the option of an all-egg liquid. You can use the leftover egg when making ravioli to brush the pasta sheets (see page 122). If you want to use fewer eggs, you can use 2 eggs plus 1/4 cup water.

YIELD: *16 ounces, 4 servings*

1 1/4 cups semolina flour   4 large eggs
1 1/4 cups all-purpose flour

Combine flours in pasta machine bowl. Mix 1 minute, until blended.

Lightly beat eggs together in a measuring cup. There should be 2/3 to 3/4 cup.

With pasta machine running, slowly add 1/2 cup of the eggs over a period of about 3 minutes. Let machine continue to mix another minute. The dough should consist of lumps the size of peas and walnut halves. If it seems too dry, gradually add more egg, 1/2 tablespoon at a time. If it seems too wet, add more semolina flour, 1 tablespoon at a time.

When the dough is the proper consistency, extrude according to the manufacturer's instructions.

Store pasta or cook immediately in boiling water 2 to 6 minutes.

Egg-White Pasta

This low-cholesterol pasta has the chewier texture of pasta made with eggs. You may use egg whites or an egg substitute product. However, the pasta is less flexible than all egg or water and oil pasta, so it is not the best one to use for filled pastas.

YIELD: *16 ounces, 4 servings*

1 1/4 cups semolina flour   5 large egg whites
1 1/4 cups all-purpose flour

Combine flours in pasta machine bowl. Mix 1 minute, until blended.

Lightly beat egg whites together in a measuring cup. There should be 1/2 to 2/3 cup.

With pasta machine running, slowly add 1/2 cup of the egg whites over a period of about 3 minutes. Let machine continue to mix another minute. The dough should consist of lumps the size of peas and walnut halves. If it seems too dry, gradually add more egg white, 1/2 tablespoon at a time. If it seems too wet, add more semolina flour, 1 tablespoon at a time.

When the dough is the proper consistency, extrude according to the manufacturer's instructions.

Store pasta or cook immediately in boiling water 2 to 6 minutes.

Water and Oil Pasta

This is the pasta to make if you don't want to eat eggs at all. Use it as a model for pasta made with any other liquid—wine, juice, etc. The texture is not quite as chewy as that of pasta made with whole eggs or egg whites, but it has a pleasing texture and flavor. It is very flexible and easy to use for making filled pastas.

YIELD: *16 ounces, 4 servings*

1 1/4 cups semolina flour
1 1/4 cups all-purpose flour

1/2 to 2/3 cup water
1 tablespoon olive oil

Combine flours in pasta machine bowl. Mix 1 minute, until blended.

Mix together 1/2 cup water and oil. With pasta machine running, slowly add 1/2 cup of the water mixture over a period of about 3 minutes. Let machine continue to mix another minute. The dough should consist of lumps the size of peas and walnut halves. If it seems too dry, gradually add water, 1/2 tablespoon at a time. If it seems too wet, add more semolina flour, 1 tablespoon at a time.

When the dough is the proper consistency, extrude according to the manufacturer's instructions.

Store pasta or cook immediately in boiling water 2 to 6 minutes.

Gardener's Choice

The most common of flavored commercial pastas are those using vegetables, specifically tomato and spinach. But generally these green and orange pastas tend to be more colored with the vegetables than flavored. In a blind taste test, you probably could not tell the difference between spinach, tomato, and plain commercial pasta. In contrast, the homemade flavored pastas you can make in your pasta machine using fruits and vegetables are full of flavor as well as color.

In order to give produce-based pasta the most intense flavor possible, I prefer to use fruit and vegetable juices and purees exclusively, without diluting them with other ingredients. There are some exceptions, and some recipes call for egg or a little bit of oil, but in general, the vegetables themselves provide all the liquid ingredients used in the pasta.

Almost any fruit or vegetable juice or puree can be used. Try these recipes and use them for inspiration for your own fresh-from-the-garden combinations.

Spinach Pasta with Sautéed Peas & Carrots

Spinach pasta usually has no spinach flavor—it's just green. But this version uses more spinach than traditional recipes, and has a distinctive, pleasing spinach taste. You don't need to puree the spinach before adding it to the flour; the kneading and extrusion process of the machine does that while making the pasta. It goes well with this twist on the childhood combination of peas and carrots. This pasta works well with any die.

Other recommended accompaniments: Green Bean–Red Onion Sauce (page 55), Lamb and Chickpea Stew (page 117), Lemony Chard, Leeks, and Currants (page 95), Pesto (page 53).

Makes 6 servings.

Spinach Pasta

YIELD: *24 ounces*

1 (10-ounce) package frozen
   chopped spinach
1 egg, lightly beaten

2 cups semolina flour
2 cups all-purpose flour

Cook spinach according to package instructions. Drain spinach, squeezing out as much excess liquid as possible, using your hands or pressing against the side of a sieve. Save the liquid in case you need to add more liquid to the pasta mixture later. Using a fork, mix egg with drained spinach.

Combine flours in pasta machine bowl. Mix 1 minute, until blended.

With pasta machine running, slowly add spinach mixture over a period of 3 minutes. Use a spatula to help it go through the opening in the machine's lid. Let machine continue to mix another minute. The dough should consist of lumps the size of peas and walnut halves. If it seems too dry, gradually add reserved spinach liquid, 1/2 tablespoon at a time. If it seems too wet, add more semolina flour, 1 tablespoon at a time.

When the dough is the proper consistency, extrude according to the manufacturer's instructions.

When the peas and carrots are almost ready, cook pasta in boiling water 2 to 6 minutes. Drain pasta and place in a large bowl.

Sautéed Peas & Carrots

YIELD: *6 servings*

1 tablespoon olive oil
4 medium carrots, peeled and
    thinly sliced
1 cup fresh or thawed frozen green
    peas
2 tablespoons fresh chives or 1
    green onion, white and green
    parts, thinly sliced

1/8 teaspoon salt
1/4 teaspoon freshly ground black
    pepper
4 ounces goat cheese, crumbled

Heat olive oil in a large nonstick skillet over medium heat. Add carrots and sauté, stirring occasionally, until tender, about 7 minutes. Add peas and cook until heated through, about 2 minutes. Remove from heat and add chives, salt, and black pepper, stirring to mix. Set aside.

Add goat cheese to hot pasta and stir to coat pasta with cheese. Add carrot mixture and stir to distribute. Serve immediately.

Tomato Pasta with Edam Cheese Sauce

This tomato pasta is more than just a pretty color. It also has a pleasing tomato flavor. Any shape works well with this versatile pasta, from angel hair to lasagne, as well as macaroni and ziti; for this sauce I recommend the macaroni, penne, or ziti dies. I like the tomato pasta as a base for this amazingly quick and easy stovetop macaroni and cheese.

Other recommended accompaniments: Creamy Roasted Tomato Sauce (page 177), Fresh Fennel–Anchovy Sauté (page 65), Niçoise Mix (page 99), Roasted Tomato and Corn Salsa (page 77).

Makes 6 servings.

Tomato Pasta

YIELD: *24 ounces*

1 (6-ounce) can tomato paste
1 egg, lightly beaten
2 cups semolina flour

2 cups all-purpose flour
Water, as needed

Blend tomato paste with egg.

Combine flours in pasta machine bowl. Mix 1 minute, until blended.

With pasta machine running, slowly add tomato mixture over a period of 3 minutes. Let machine continue to mix another minute. The dough should consist of lumps the size of peas and walnut halves. If it seems too dry, gradually add water, 1/2 tablespoon at a time. If it seems too wet, add more semolina flour, 1 tablespoon at a time.

When the dough is the proper consistency, extrude according to the manufacturer's instructions.

Cook pasta in boiling water 2 to 6 minutes. Drain pasta and place in a large bowl.

Edam Cheese Sauce

YIELD: *about 2 cups*

1 1/2 cups milk
6 ounces Edam cheese, shredded
1/8 teaspoon freshly ground black
    pepper

1/4 teaspoon dried basil

Heat milk over medium heat until bubbles begin to form around edge. Add shredded Edam cheese and stir until cheese is melted and mixture is smooth. Remove from heat and stir in pepper and basil. Toss with pasta and serve immediately.

Sun-Dried Tomato Pasta with Sun-Dried Tomato Pesto

Sun-dried tomatoes have a unique, intense flavor unlike that of fresh or canned tomatoes. I prefer using sun-dried tomatoes packed dry, not those packed in oil. This enables you to make a pesto lower in fat, because you control how much oil goes into it. Dry sun-dried tomatoes are available in the produce section of supermarkets and in the bulk section of natural food stores. The pesto also makes a great spread for sandwiches. This recipe goes well with the fettuccine or linguine dies.

Other recommended accompaniments: Chunky Tomato Sauce (page 171), Cucumber Sauce (page 51), Pesto (page 53), Rosemary-Garlic Sauce (page 167).

Makes 4 servings.

Sun-Dried Tomato Pasta

YIELD: *16 ounces*

4 ounces sun-dried tomatoes, not
    oil-packed
2 cups boiling water
2 tablespoons olive oil

1/4 teaspoon salt
1 1/4 cups all-purpose flour
1 1/4 cups semolina flour

Pour boiling water over sun-dried tomatoes and let steep 15 to 30 minutes or until softened. Drain, reserving liquid. Place tomatoes in a blender or food processor with olive oil and 1/4 cup of the reserved liquid. Blend until smooth, scraping down the sides of the bowl as needed.

Pour sun-dried tomato puree into a 2-cup measuring cup. There should be about 1 1/3 cups puree. Set aside 1 cup for the pesto and return 1/3 cup puree to the blender or food processor.

Add 1/3 cup reserved soaking liquid and 1/4 teaspoon salt to puree in blender and blend until the texture of thin tomato paste.

Combine flours in pasta machine bowl. Mix 1 minute, until blended.

With pasta machine running, slowly add thinned sun-dried tomato puree over a period of 3 minutes. Stop the machine as needed and break up clumps of puree so that it mixes better with the flour. Let machine continue to mix another minute. The dough should consist of lumps the size of peas and walnut halves. If it seems too dry, gradually add reserved soaking water, 1/2 tablespoon at a time. If it seems too wet, add more semolina flour, 1 tablespoon at a time.

When the dough is the proper consistency, extrude according to the manufacturer's instructions.

When the pesto is ready, cook pasta in boiling water 1 to 4 minutes. Drain pasta and place in a large bowl.

Sun-Dried Tomato Pesto

YIELD: *1 1/3 cups*

2 cloves garlic, peeled
1/4 cup walnuts
1 cup reserved sun-dried tomato
    puree (from above)
1 tablespoon packed chopped fresh
    basil or 1 teaspoon dried basil

2 tablespoons olive oil
1/4 cup reserved tomato soaking
    liquid (from above)
1/4 cup grated Parmesan cheese
    (optional)

With food processor running, drop in garlic cloves and walnuts to mince. Stop machine and add sun-dried tomato puree, basil, olive oil, and tomato soaking liquid; puree until smooth. (The sauce may be frozen at this point. Defrost when ready to use and then add cheese, if desired.) Stir in cheese, if using.

To serve, pour about 1/2 to 2/3 cup of sauce over cooked pasta and toss to coat thoroughly. Reserve remaining sauce for use as a sandwich spread or freeze for up to 1 month.

Roasted Red Pepper Pasta with Roasted Red Pepper Sauce

Roasted red bell peppers have a wonderful, smoky flavor. This pasta gets a double dose of that taste, with peppers in and on the pasta. The cottage cheese provides a contrasting taste and texture. There will be extra sauce, which will keep in the refrigerator up to a week or in the freezer for three months. This pasta works well with any die.

Other recommended accompaniments: Cilantro-Lime Pesto (page 59), Herb-Roasted Vegetables (page 49), Poached Salmon and Spinach Beurre Blanc (page 101), Roasted Peppers and Herbs (page 141).

Makes 4 servings.

Roasted Red Pepper Pasta

YIELD: *16 ounces*

6 red bell peppers
2 tablespoons extra-virgin olive oil
1/2 teaspoon salt
1/2 teaspoon freshly ground black
    pepper

1 1/4 cups semolina flour
1 1/4 cups all-purpose flour

Roast bell peppers: Preheat broiler. Line a baking sheet with heavy-duty foil and lightly brush with oil. Cut each bell pepper in half, removing seeds and membranes. Place bell pepper halves, cut side down, on foil-lined baking sheet and broil until skin turns black, about 10 minutes. If all bell peppers do not fit on baking sheet, cook in two batches. Check after 5 minutes and rotate baking sheet, if necessary, to ensure even broiling. When skins are black, remove from oven and let sit a few minutes until cool enough to handle. Remove and discard skins from bell peppers.

Chop bell peppers coarsely and puree in a blender or food processor with olive oil, salt, and black pepper.

Reserve 3/4 cup pureed bell pepper mixture for pasta and set remaining pureed mixture aside for sauce.

Combine flours in pasta machine bowl. Mix 1 minute, until blended.

With pasta machine running, slowly add 1/2 cup of the pureed bell peppers over a period of about 3 minutes. Let machine continue to mix another minute. The dough should consist of lumps the size of peas and walnut halves. If it seems too dry, gradually add more pureed bell peppers, 1/2 tablespoon at a time. If it seems too wet, add more semolina flour, 1 tablespoon at a time.

When the dough is the proper consistency, extrude according to the manufacturer's instructions.

Cook pasta in boiling water 2 to 6 minutes. Drain and place in a large bowl.

Roasted Red Pepper Sauce

YIELD: *about 1 1/4 cups*

Remaining pureed roasted bell   1/2 cup cottage cheese
    pepper mixture (from above)

Mix cooked pasta with 1 cup of puree to coat thoroughly. Stir in cottage cheese. Add additional puree to taste.

Variation

Grill bell peppers. Place bell pepper halves skin side down on grill rack and grill until skins turn black. Proceed as above.

Beet Pasta with Rosy Vegetable Sauce

The color of beets has always appealed to me. I find it incredible that such a vibrant color exists naturally in nature. Although some of the vividness of the pink gets lost in cooking the pasta, the sauce makes up for it. The sauce is filled with magenta-colored vegetables. Horseradish adds a pleasing kick.

This pasta works well with any die.

Other recommended accompaniments: Beurre Rouge (page 163), Cucumber Sauce (page 51), Mustard Vinaigrette and Corned Beef (page 89), Smoked Trout Sauce (page 61).

Makes 6 servings.

Beet Pasta

YIELD: *20 ounces*

1 (15-ounce) can sliced beets
1 1/2 cups semolina flour

1 1/2 cups all-purpose flour

Place 16 of the beet slices in a blender or food processor and puree, reserving remaining beets. Pour puree into a measuring cup. There should be about 3/4 cup.

Combine flours in pasta machine bowl. Mix 1 minute, until blended.

With pasta machine running, slowly add 1/2 cup beet puree over a period of 4 to 5 minutes. Stop the machine as needed and break up clumps of puree so that it mixes better with the flour. Let machine continue to mix another minute. The dough should consist of lumps the size of peas and walnut halves. If it seems too dry, gradually add more puree, 1/2 tablespoon at a time. If it seems too wet, add more semolina flour, 1 tablespoon at a time.

When the dough is the proper consistency, extrude according to the manufacturer's instructions.

When the sauce is almost ready, cook pasta in boiling water 1 to 4 minutes. Drain pasta and place in a large bowl.

Rosy Vegetable Sauce

YIELD: *6 servings*

1 tablespoon olive oil
1 medium red onion, diced
3 radishes, minced
2 cups loosely packed julienned
    radicchio leaves
Remaining beet slices (from above),
    diced
1 teaspoon prepared horseradish

1/2 teaspoon balsamic vinegar
3/4 teaspoon salt
1/4 teaspoon freshly ground black
    pepper
1/2 cup milk
1 cup sour cream
1/4 cup minced fresh parsley

Heat olive oil in a medium skillet over medium-high heat. Add onion and cook until tender, about 10 minutes.

Add radishes and cook 2 to 3 minutes, then add radicchio. Cook, stirring, until radicchio wilts, about 5 minutes. Add beets, horseradish, and balsamic vinegar. Add salt and pepper and stir to distribute. Reduce heat to low.

In a measuring cup, mix together the milk and sour cream and add to the vegetables. Cook over low heat, stirring constantly, until warmed through. Do not boil or mixture may curdle.

Add drained pasta and stir to coat thoroughly. Sprinkle with minced parsley and serve immediately.

Carrot Pasta with Curried Lentil Soup

Carrot juice gives this pasta a noticeable carrot flavor, not to mention healthy vitamin A. Buy the carrot juice or make it yourself using a juicer. I like making this pasta with the spaghetti die and cutting the strands about 6 inches long—long enough to look nice but not too long to be unmanageable when eating.

Garam masala is an Indian spice combination that usually includes cinnamon, cumin, and several other spices. It is available from Indian markets. If unavailable, regular curry powder may be used.

This recipe makes a lot of soup and is a terrific hearty winter one-dish meal. It makes great leftovers, but note that both the pasta and the lentils continue to expand. By the next day the soup will be much thicker, more like a stew.

Other recommended accompaniments: Beef 'n' Beer Goulash (page 115), Chicken Mole Sauce (page 69), Sautéed Peas & Carrots (page 19), Spicy Peanut Sauce (page 75).

Makes 10 to 12 servings.

Carrot Pasta

YIELD: *16 ounces*

1 1/4 cups semolina flour
1 1/4 cups all-purpose flour

About 1/2 cup carrot juice

Combine flours in pasta machine bowl. Mix 1 minute, until blended.

With pasta machine running, slowly add 1/2 cup carrot juice over a period of 3 minutes. Let machine continue to mix another minute. The dough should consist of lumps the size of peas and walnut halves. If it seems too dry, gradually add more juice, 1/2 tablespoon at a time. If it seems too wet, add more semolina flour, 1 tablespoon at a time. Break up larger clumps of dough with a rubber spatula or knife to ensure even incorporation of the liquid.

When the dough is the proper consistency, extrude according to the manufacturer's instructions.

Cook pasta in boiling water 4 to 6 minutes or in boiling soup as directed on page 29.

Curried Lentil Soup

YIELD: *about 4 quarts*

7 cups Vegetable Stock (page 173)
    or Chicken Stock (page 107)
7 cups water
1 1/2 cups lentils, sorted and rinsed
1 large onion, finely chopped
2 stalks celery, thinly sliced

2 medium carrots, thinly sliced
2 tablespoons grated ginger root
3/4 teaspoon salt
1 teaspoon garam masala or curry
    powder
Cilantro sprigs, for garnish

Combine stock and water in a large stockpot. Add lentils, onion, celery, carrots, and ginger. Cover and bring to a boil over high heat, about 20 minutes. Reduce heat and simmer until lentils are tender, about 45 minutes.

Return to a boil and add pasta. Cook 4 to 6 minutes, until pasta is just tender to the bite. Serve in deep soup bowls, garnished with cilantro sprigs.

Roasted Butternut Squash Pasta with Coconut-Squash Sauce

Because of the sweetness of the squash, this pasta tends to cook a little faster than others; check for doneness after 1 minute. This pasta works well with the fettuccine or linguine dies.

For the sauce, use coconut milk, not cream of coconut. Coconut milk can be found in Asian markets and in the international food section of the supermarket.

Other recommended accompaniments: Herb-Roasted Vegetables (page 49), Indian Braised Potatoes (page 71), Indian Karhi Sauce and Chickpeas (page 87), Lemon-Ginger Sauce (page 128).

Makes 6 servings.

Butternut Squash Pasta

YIELD: 20 ounces

1 small butternut squash (about
    2 pounds)
1 small red onion

1 1/2 cups semolina flour
1 1/2 cups all-purpose flour

Preheat oven to 450F (230C). Line a baking sheet with foil and lightly oil foil. Rinse squash and cut in half lengthwise. Scoop out and discard seeds. Remove ends and skin from onion and cut in half. Fit onion halves into the scooped-out seed cavity of each squash half. Place squash and onion halves, cut side down, on prepared baking sheet and roast 40 to 45 minutes, until soft.

Set onion aside for sauce. Scoop squash flesh out of skin into a blender or food processor and puree until smooth. Reserve 3/4 cup pureed squash mixture for pasta and set remaining pureed mixture aside for sauce.

Combine flours in pasta machine bowl. Mix 1 minute, until blended.

With pasta machine running, slowly add 1/2 cup squash puree over a period of 4 to 5 minutes. Stop the machine as needed and break up clumps of puree so that it mixes better with the flour. Let machine continue to mix another minute. The dough should consist of lumps the size of peas and walnut halves. If it seems too dry, gradually add more puree, 1/2 tablespoon at a time. If it seems too wet, add more semolina flour, 1 tablespoon at a time.

When the dough is the proper consistency, extrude according to the manufacturer's instructions.

When sauce is almost ready, cook pasta in boiling water 1 to 4 minutes. Drain pasta and place in a large bowl.

Coconut-Squash Sauce

YIELD: *6 servings*

1 roasted onion (from above), coarsely chopped
1/2 cup coconut milk
1/2 cup vegetable stock or chicken broth
About 3/4 to 1 cup of remaining pureed roasted squash (from above)
2 teaspoons freshly squeezed lime juice (about 1/2 small lime)
1/8 teaspoon salt or to taste

1/8 teaspoon freshly ground black pepper
2 tablespoons butter
1 leek, white part only, rinsed well and thinly sliced
1 red bell pepper, diced
4 cups diced butternut squash [about 1 (2-pound) squash]
1 cup diced cooked chicken
1/4 cup chopped fresh cilantro

Add onion, coconut milk, stock, squash puree, and lime juice to a blender or food processor and puree until smooth. The mixture should be thick but pourable. Add salt and pepper to taste. There should be 1 3/4 to 2 cups sauce.

Melt butter in a large saucepan over medium heat. Add leeks and sauté until translucent, 5 to 7 minutes. Add bell pepper and cook until bell pepper softens slightly, about 2 minutes. Add diced squash and increase heat to medium-high. Cook, stirring, 3 minutes, then cover the pan and cook over medium heat 5 minutes. Remove cover; squash should be slightly soft. Increase heat to medium-high again and sauté, stirring frequently, until squash is beginning to soften and stick to the pan. If necessary, reduce heat to avoid burning. Add chicken and heat over medium-low heat until hot. Add the reserved 2 cups coconut-squash mixture and cook, stirring, until combined and hot. Add sauce mixture to pasta, stirring to mix thoroughly. Serve immediately, garnished with chopped cilantro.

Asparagus Pasta with Asparagus, Leeks, and Red Peppers

Asparagus is the first sign of spring in the produce section, and I love it. The puree yields a lovely pale green pasta that is complemented by the bright green asparagus tips. The smokiness of the roasted red bell peppers combined with the sweetness of slow-cooked leeks and the tang of lemon juice makes a delightful combination. This pasta works well with any die.

Other recommended accompaniments: Asparagus-Mushroom Sauce (page 131), Creamed Leeks (page 159), Niçoise Mix (page 99), Vegetable Soup (page 173).

Makes 4 servings.

Asparagus Pasta

YIELD: *16 ounces*

1 3/4 to 2 pounds asparagus
1 teaspoon olive oil
1 1/4 cups all-purpose flour

1 1/4 cups semolina flour
Water, as needed

Cook the asparagus: Break off the woody ends. To do this, feel along the bottom of the asparagus stem and bend until it breaks easily. Set the ends aside. Cut the tips from the asparagus and place in a separate bowl. Place the stems in a microwave-safe pan, cover with microwave-safe plastic wrap, and cook on HIGH 5 minutes. Check for doneness. Be careful when removing plastic wrap, as the steam is very hot. Stems should hold their shape but be soft. If they are not quite soft, cook on HIGH 1 minute. Let stand, covered, a few minutes while you cook the tips. Place tips in a microwave-safe bowl, cover with plastic wrap, and cook on HIGH 1 to 2 minutes until bright green but still firm. Remove plastic wrap immediately and set asparagus tips aside for sauce.

Puree the stems with olive oil in a food processor until very smooth. There should be about 1 cup; reserve 1/2 cup for sauce.

Combine flours in pasta machine bowl. Mix 1 minute, until blended.

With pasta machine running, slowly add 1/2 cup asparagus puree over a period of 4 to 5 minutes. Stop the machine as needed and break up clumps of puree so that it mixes better with the flour. Let machine continue to mix another minute. The dough should consist of lumps the size of peas and walnut halves. If it seems too dry, gradually add water, 1/2 tablespoon at a time. If it seems too wet, add more semolina flour, 1 tablespoon at a time. Be careful; this dough seems to go from too dry to too wet in a matter of seconds.

When the dough is the proper consistency, extrude according to the manufacturer's instructions.

When the vegetables are almost ready, cook pasta in boiling water 2 to 6 minutes. For added asparagus flavor, put the reserved broken asparagus ends in the pasta cooking water. Drain pasta, reserving 1/2 cup cooking water, discarding asparagus ends, if using.

Asparagus, Leeks, and Red Peppers

YIELD: *4 servings*

1 tablespoon olive oil
2 cups thinly sliced leeks, white and
    pale green parts only (about
    4 medium leeks), rinsed well
2 red bell peppers
Asparagus tips (from above)
1/2 cup asparagus puree

1/4 teaspoon salt
1/4 teaspoon freshly ground black
    pepper
1 tablespoon freshly squeezed
    lemon juice
1/2 cup pasta cooking water or
    vegetable stock

Heat olive oil in a large skillet or saucepan over medium-high heat. Add leeks and cook, stirring frequently, until softened and beginning to caramelize, about 30 minutes.

While the leeks are cooking, roast the bell peppers according to directions on page 24. When skins are blackened, remove from oven and let sit a few minutes until cool enough to handle. Peel off and discard skins; cut bell peppers into 1/2-inch pieces.

Add bell peppers and reserved asparagus tips to leeks. Cook about 3 minutes, then add asparagus puree, stirring to coat the vegetables. Add salt, pepper, and lemon juice.

Stir reserved 1/2 cup pasta cooking water into the sauce. Taste and adjust the seasonings.

Add pasta and toss to combine. Serve immediately.

Caramelized-Onion Pasta with Walnut–Goat Cheese Sauce

The onions are cooked slowly until their sugars melt and give the onions a wonderful, intriguing sweetness. Balsamic vinegar intensifies this flavor. The onions may be prepared in advance and kept refrigerated up to 3 days. Vidalias, a sweet onion from Georgia, are my favorite kind of onion to use in this recipe; they seem to caramelize more easily and to become the most meltingly soft. They are available in the spring and fall. This pasta works well with the fettuccine die.

Other recommended accompaniments: Chestnut-Mushroom Delight (page 85), Miso Broth with Wasabi Drizzle (page 81), Rosemary-Garlic Sauce (page 167), Stir-Fried Vegetables (page 63).

Makes 4 servings.

Caramelized-Onion Pasta

YIELD: *18 ounces*

8 cups diced onions [4 to 5 large
    onions (3 pounds)], preferably
    Vidalia
1 tablespoon olive oil
1 tablespoon plus 1 teaspoon
    balsamic vinegar

1/8 teaspoon salt
1 1/4 cups semolina flour
1 1/4 cups all-purpose flour
1/2 cup water

Heat olive oil in a large skillet over medium-high heat. Add onions and stir. Reduce heat to medium and cook, uncovered, 10 minutes, stirring occasionally, until onions soften slightly. Cover, increase heat to medium high, and cook 20 minutes to soften the onions and steam them slightly, making them softer when caramelized.

Remove cover and cook over medium-high heat until liquid begins to evaporate and onions begin to turn pale gold, about 15 minutes. Watch carefully so onions do not become too brown and burn. When liquid begins to evaporate, cook, stirring frequently, until onions begin to turn golden brown. Turn off heat and add the 1 tablespoon balsamic vinegar and salt, stirring to mix thoroughly. The onions should be very soft, slightly sweet, and practically melt in your mouth when you taste them. Measure 1/2 cup onions for pasta and reserve remaining onions for sauce.

Combine flours in pasta machine bowl. Mix 1 minute, until blended.

Open pasta machine lid and spoon 1/2 cup caramelized onions around the flour and mix 1 to 2 minutes. Mix remaining teaspoon balsamic vinegar with the water. With pasta machine running, slowly add about half of the vinegar-water mixture to flour over a period of about 3 minutes. Let machine continue to mix another minute. The dough should consist of lumps the size of peas and walnut halves. If it seems too dry, gradually add more water mixture, 1/2 tablespoon at a time. If it seems too wet, add more semolina flour, 1 tablespoon at a time. Be careful; this dough seems to go from too dry to too wet in a matter of seconds.

When the dough is the proper consistency, extrude according to the manufacturer's instructions.

When the sauce is almost ready, cook pasta in boiling water 2 to 6 minutes. Drain pasta and place in a large bowl.

Walnut–Goat Cheese Sauce

YIELD: *4 servings*

1 cup caramelized onions (from above)

1 cup chicken broth or vegetable stock

2 ounces chèvre (goat cheese), crumbled

1/3 cup coarsely chopped walnuts, toasted (see Note, below)

Combine caramelized onions and broth in a medium saucepan and cook over high heat until sauce boils. Reduce heat to low and simmer 3 to 4 minutes. Mixture will thicken slightly.

Toss onion mixture with cooked pasta, then sprinkle half the cheese and the walnuts on pasta and toss to mix until cheese melts. Place on individual plates and top each serving with remaining goat cheese.

Note To toast walnuts, place walnuts in a small, dry, heavy-bottomed skillet over low heat and heat about 5 minutes, until they smell toasted and fragrant.

Microwave: Place walnuts on a microwave-safe plate and cook on HIGH 3 minutes. Walnuts should smell toasted; if not, cook on HIGH 1 to 2 minutes more.

Roasted Garlic Pasta with Roasted Garlic Sauce and Peas

The preparation steps for this pasta take some time, although they are simple to do. The garlic puree can be prepared up to 3 days in advance. The result is sweet, heady, piquant garlic pasta. The garlic puree is also used in the sauce, so the sauce takes only minutes to prepare. This pasta works well with any die.

Other recommended accompaniments: Garlicky Chile con Carne (page 120), Kale, Leeks, and Potatoes (page 79), Puttanesca Sauce (page 139), Smoked Trout Sauce (page 61).

Makes 6 servings.

Roasted Garlic Pasta

YIELD: *20 ounces*

4 to 5 heads garlic
About 2 cups milk
2 teaspoons butter

1/4 cup white wine
1 1/2 cups semolina flour
1 1/2 cups all-purpose flour

Preheat oven to 400F (205C). Separate the garlic cloves, removing any skin that comes off easily. Place in a small saucepan and cover with 2 cups milk. Heat over medium heat until the milk is just barely simmering and cook garlic 10 minutes or until garlic cloves are slightly softened.

Butter a medium casserole dish or soufflé dish. Drain garlic, reserving milk. Place garlic cloves in prepared dish. Cut butter into small pieces and dot garlic with butter. Cover casserole with foil and bake 30 minutes or until garlic is golden in patches and soft to the touch.

Let garlic cool slightly, until cool enough to handle. If garlic cloves still have skin on them, hold cloves by end that was attached to the head and squeeze out the garlic into a clean bowl, separating flesh from the skin. If cloves were completely peeled before roasting, simply pinch off hard root end of each clove.

Pour reserved milk into the soufflé dish, stirring to scrape up any bits of caramelized garlic, and place dish in oven 10 minutes to give the milk more of a garlic flavor.

Puree the garlic by hand with a fork or preferably with an immersion blender, as this makes the smoothest sauce and is easiest to clean, or use a regular blender. There should be about 1/3 cup garlic puree. Add half the heated milk and blend or stir until smooth. Add remaining milk and blend or stir until smooth. Pour into a 2-cup glass measuring cup. If less than 2 cups, add enough milk to make 2 cups. Measure 1/2 cup to use for the pasta and set aside the remaining 1 1/2 cups for the sauce. Mix the white wine with the 1/2 cup garlic-milk mixture.

Combine flours in pasta machine bowl. Mix 1 minute, until blended.

With pasta machine running, slowly add most of the garlic mixture to the flour, reserving a few tablespoons, over a period of 3 minutes. Let machine continue to mix another minute. The dough should consist of lumps the size of peas and walnut halves. If it seems too dry, gradually add garlic mixture, 1/2 tablespoon at a time. If it seems too wet, add more semolina flour, 1 tablespoon at a time.

When the dough is the proper consistency, extrude according to the manufacturer's instructions.

When the sauce is almost ready, cook pasta in boiling water 2 to 6 minutes. Drain pasta and place in a large bowl.

Roasted Garlic Sauce and Peas

YIELD: *about 1 1/2 cups*

1 1/2 cups garlic-milk mixture (from above)
2 tablespoons regular or low-fat cream cheese
1/4 teaspoon salt

1/4 teaspoon freshly ground black pepper
3 dashes Tabasco sauce
1 cup cooked green peas

Heat garlic-milk mixture in a small saucepan over low heat. Cut cream cheese into small pieces, add to saucepan, and cook, stirring occasionally, until cheese is melted and mixed into the garlic mixture. Stir in salt, pepper, and Tabasco sauce. Taste and adjust seasonings. (Sauce may be prepared in advance up to this point and refrigerated up to 2 days.) Add green peas and cook until heated through.

Toss sauce with cooked pasta and serve immediately.

Mushroom Pasta with Mushroom-Herb Pesto

Pesto means "paste," and in this sauce, pureed mushrooms are cooked in a thick, savory sauce. The double dose of mushrooms both in and on the pasta yields a delicious earthy flavor—a perfect autumn dish. Use this buff-colored pasta to make the mushroom ravioli on page 130. This pasta works well with any die.

Other recommended accompaniments: Chestnut-Mushroom Delight (page 85), Miso Broth with Wasabi Drizzle (page 81), Rosemary-Garlic Sauce (page 167), Stir-Fried Vegetables (page 63).

Makes 4 servings.

Mushroom Pasta

YIELD: *16 ounces*

1 pound mushrooms, cleaned and
    stems trimmed
1 tablespoon olive oil
1/4 teaspoon salt

1 1/4 cups semolina flour
1 1/4 cups all-purpose flour
White wine or water as needed

Process mushrooms in a food processor until pureed.

Heat 1 tablespoon olive oil in a medium skillet over medium-high heat. Add pureed mushrooms and stir. Sprinkle salt over mushrooms and stir to mix. Reduce heat to medium and cook mushrooms about 10 minutes or until moisture is released and mushrooms smell cooked. Pour into a 2-cup glass measuring cup. There should be about 1 1/2 cups. Let cool slightly. Measure 1/2 cup to use for the pasta and set aside the remaining 1 cup for the pesto.

Combine flours in pasta machine bowl. Mix 1 minute, until blended.

With pasta machine running, slowly add 1/2 cup mushroom puree over a period of 3 minutes. Let machine continue to mix another minute. The dough should consist of lumps the size of peas and walnut halves. If it seems too dry, gradually add white wine or water, 1/2 tablespoon at a time. If it seems too wet, add more semolina flour, 1 tablespoon at a time.

When the dough is the proper consistency, extrude according to the manufacturer's instructions.

When the sauce is almost ready, cook pasta in boiling water 4 to 6 minutes. Drain pasta, toss with remaining 1 tablespoon olive oil and place in a large bowl.

Mushroom-Herb Pesto

YIELD: *about 2/3 cup*

2 tablespoons olive oil
1 bunch green onions, both white
    and green parts, minced
1 cup mushroom puree (from above)
1/8 teaspoon salt

1 1/2 tablespoons fresh lemon juice
1/4 teaspoon freshly ground black
    pepper
1/2 cup minced fresh cilantro
Paprika

Heat olive oil in a medium skillet over medium heat. Add green onions and cook until soft, about 10 minutes.

Add mushroom puree and salt and sauté over medium-high heat until most of the liquid has evaporated. Add lemon juice and stir, scraping up any bits of the mushroom mixture stuck to the pan. Sauté until the liquid has evaporated, then remove from heat. Immediately add pepper and cilantro and mix well. Toss with cooked pasta, stirring well to coat evenly. Serve in shallow bowls, sprinkled with paprika.

Apple Pasta with Apple, Leeks, and Brie

Leeks and apples make wonderful partners, complemented here by bits of creamy Brie. This pasta also makes terrific noodle kugel (page 148). It is best suited to wider noodles, such as fettuccine and papardelle. The sweetness of the apple concentrate helps the pasta to cook quickly, so watch it carefully once you add it to the boiling water.

Other recommended accompaniments: Creamed Leeks (page 159), Curried Lentil Soup (page 29), Maple-Walnut Sauce (page 93), Sherried Apples and Pecans (page 169).

Makes 4 servings.

Apple Pasta

YIELD: *16 ounces*

1 1/4 cups semolina flour
1 1/4 cups all-purpose flour
About 1/3 cup frozen apple juice
    concentrate, thawed

1 egg, lightly beaten

Combine flours in machine bowl. Mix 1 minute, until blended.

Stir together 1/3 cup apple juice and egg. With pasta machine running, slowly add egg mixture over a period of 3 minutes, reserving 2 tablespoons. Let machine continue to mix another minute. The dough should consist of lumps the size of peas and walnut halves. If it seems too dry, gradually add remaining egg mixture, then apple juice concentrate, 1/2 tablespoon at a time. If it seems too wet, add more semolina flour, 1 tablespoon at a time.

When the dough is the proper consistency, extrude according to the manufacturer's instructions.

When the apple and leeks are almost ready, cook pasta in boiling water 1 to 4 minutes. Drain pasta and place in a large bowl.

Apple, Leeks, and Brie

YIELD: *4 servings*

1 tablespoon unsalted butter
2 cups thinly sliced leeks, white part
    and a few inches of pale green
    (about 4 medium leeks), rinsed
    well
1 Granny Smith apple, peeled,
    cored, and chopped into
    1/2-inch pieces

2 tablespoons Calvados or apple
    brandy
1/8 teaspoon salt
1/4 teaspoon freshly ground black
    pepper
2 ounces Brie, cut into 1/2-inch
    chunks

Melt butter in a large skillet over medium heat. Add leeks and cook 5 to 8 minutes, until leeks are translucent. Add apple and sauté until hot, about 2 to 3 minutes. Add 1 tablespoon Calvados and stir to deglaze. Mix in salt and pepper.

Add half the Brie and stir until it melts into the leeks and apples. Add remaining tablespoon Calvados and stir until alcohol evaporates.

Add pasta to the leek mixture and stir to mix. Add remaining Brie and stir briefly. Serve immediately.

Orange-Basil Pasta with Orange Butter Sauce

Orange juice makes this pasta slightly sweet, and basil adds an unusual savory touch. The accompanying sauce is so simple to make, and absolutely delicious. Try this with a side of asparagus or broccoli. This recipe works well with the fettuccine or linguine dies.

Other recommended accompaniments: Coconut-Squash Sauce (page 31), Pesto (page 53), Sherried Apples and Pecans (page 169), Sole Amandine (page 105).

Makes 4 servings.

Orange-Basil Pasta

YIELD: *16 ounces*

1 1/4 cups semolina flour
1 1/4 cups all-purpose flour
2 tablespoons chopped fresh basil or
    2 teaspoons dried

Grated zest of 1/2 orange (about
    1 teaspoon)
1/2 to 2/3 cup orange juice

Combine flours in pasta machine bowl. Mix 1 minute, until blended. Add basil and orange zest and mix 1 minute.

With pasta machine running, slowly add 1/2 cup orange juice over a period of 3 minutes. Let machine continue to mix another minute. The dough should consist of lumps the size of peas and walnut halves. If it seems too dry, gradually add more juice, 1/2 tablespoon at a time. If it seems too wet, add more semolina flour, 1 tablespoon at a time.

When the dough is the proper consistency, extrude according to the manufacturer's instructions.

When the sauce is ready, cook pasta in boiling water 2 to 6 minutes. Drain pasta and place in a large bowl.

Orange Butter Sauce

YIELD: *about 3/4 cup*

1/4 cup butter
1/2 cup orange juice

Fresh basil leaves, for garnish

Melt butter in a small saucepan over medium heat and cook until it is slightly browned. Whisk in orange juice and stir until combined. Mixture will foam up a little, but keep stirring.

Spoon over cooked pasta and toss to combine. Serve garnished with fresh basil leaves.

This sauce will keep, refrigerated, several days. To use, heat until the butter is melted.

Grapefruit Pasta with Watercress, Fresh Mozzarella, and Lime Vinaigrette

This refreshing pasta salad was inspired by a number of favorite recipes that combine greens and citrus flavors. The lime vinaigrette is adapted from a recipe in The Tassajara Recipe Book *(Random House, 1985), and it is an intriguing, wonderful combination of flavors. I like using pink grapefruit for the pale pink tint it gives the pasta and the sunny color it adds to the salad. Since this pasta is used for a salad, I recommend extruding it into bite-size shapes, such as penne, ziti, or macaroni.*

Other recommended accompaniments: Honey-Lemon Chicken (page 111), Lime-Pistachio Sauce (page 133), Pear Vinaigrette and Greens (page 137), Sole Amandine (page 105).

Makes 4 servings.

Grapefruit Pasta

YIELD: *16 ounces*

1 1/4 cups semolina flour
1 1/4 cups all-purpose flour

Grated zest of 1 grapefruit
Juice from 1 grapefruit (about 2/3 cup)

Combine flours in pasta machine bowl. Mix 1 minute, until blended. Add grated grapefruit zest and mix 1 minute.

With pasta machine running, slowly add 1/2 cup grapefruit juice over a period of 3 minutes. Let machine continue to mix another minute. The dough should consist of lumps the size of peas and walnut halves. If it seems too dry, gradually add more juice, 1/2 tablespoon at a time. If it seems too wet, add more semolina flour, 1 tablespoon at a time.

When the dough is the proper consistency, extrude according to the manufacturer's instructions.

Cook pasta in boiling water 2 to 6 minutes. Drain pasta and place in a large bowl.

Watercress, Fresh Mozzarella, and Lime Vinaigrette

YIELD: *4 servings*

3 bunches watercress
5 tablespoons olive oil, divided
2 teaspoons honey
1 pink grapefruit
2 oranges
Grated zest of 4 limes
1 clove garlic
1 teaspoon salt
1/2 teaspoon ground cumin
1/2 teaspoon ground coriander

1/2 teaspoon ground mustard
1/2 teaspoon paprika
Freshly squeezed juice from 2 limes
    (about 5 tablespoons)
2 tablespoons chopped fresh chives
    or 2 green onions, thinly sliced,
    both white and green parts
8 ounces fresh mozzarella, cut into
    1/2-inch pieces

Trim the thick stems from the watercress. Rinse and dry the watercress. Coarsely chop and set aside.

Toss hot pasta with 1 tablespoon of the olive oil. Drizzle with honey and toss to coat.

Cut the grapefruit in half and cut out each section using a paring or grapefruit knife. Use a spoon to scoop out the sections and any remaining flesh, and add to the pasta. Toss to combine.

Peel oranges, removing zest and white pith. Cut oranges in half and separate the sections, adding them to the pasta. Toss to combine.

Prepare the dressing: Place lime zest in a jar or other container with a tight-fitting lid. If you have a mortar and pestle, crush the garlic clove with the salt. Use the pestle to stir in cumin, coriander, mustard, and paprika. Stir in lime juice 1 tablespoon at a time. Or finely mince the garlic and place in a small bowl. Mix with salt, then cumin, coriander, mustard, and paprika. Stir in lime juice 1 tablespoon at a time.

Pour lime juice mixture into the jar with the lime zest and add remaining 4 tablespoons of olive oil. Close lid and shake jar vigorously to emulsify the dressing. Set aside.

Add the watercress, chives, and fresh mozzarella to the pasta. Pour 1/4 cup dressing over the pasta, reserving the remaining dressing. Toss to combine. Serve the salad at room temperature or chilled. If you refrigerate the salad before serving, add some of the reserved dressing, if needed.

Spice of Life

An easy way to make flavored pasta is to add a teaspoon of dried herbs or spices to any of the basic pasta recipes in the introduction. This chapter offers more intricate recipes, using creative combinations of herbs and spices, both fresh and dried.

Lemon-Parsley Pasta with Herb-Roasted Vegetables

Lemons and parsley complement each other beautifully. Fresh lemon juice and grated zest give this pasta a refreshing kick, and the parsley colors it with streaks of green. I recommend using the wider dies such as papardelle or fettuccine. It's great hot, with roasted vegetables, and it also works well for pasta salad—the vegetables are good cold too.

Other recommended accompaniments: Honey-Lemon Chicken (page 111), Lamb and Chickpea Stew (page 117), Lemony Chard, Leeks, and Currants (page 95), Sole Amandine (page 105).

Makes 4 servings.

Lemon-Parsley Pasta

YIELD: *16 ounces*

1 1/4 cups semolina flour
1 1/4 cups all-purpose flour
1/2 cup plus 2 tablespoons finely
    minced fresh parsley

Grated zest of 1 lemon
3 tablespoons fresh lemon juice
About 3 tablespoons water

Combine flours in pasta machine bowl. Mix 1 minute, until blended. Add parsley and lemon zest and mix 1 minute.

Stir together lemon juice and 3 tablespoons water. With pasta machine running, slowly add juice mixture over a period of 3 minutes. Let machine continue to mix another minute. The dough should consist of lumps the size of peas and walnut halves. If it seems too dry, gradually add more water, 1/2 tablespoon at a time. If it seems too wet, add more semolina flour, 1 tablespoon at a time.

When the dough is the proper consistency, extrude according to the manufacturer's instructions.

When the vegetables are ready, cook pasta in boiling water 2 to 6 minutes. Drain pasta and place in a large bowl.

Herb-Roasted Vegetables

YIELD: *4 servings*

1 onion, coarsely chopped
1 red bell pepper, cut into 1 x 1/2-inch
    pieces
1 yellow bell pepper, cut into
    1 x 1/2-inch pieces
12 ounces mushrooms, stems
    trimmed and cut into quarters

1 teaspoon olive oil
1 teaspoon ground cumin
1 teaspoon dried oregano
1/4 teaspoon freshly ground black
    pepper
1/8 teaspoon salt

Preheat oven to 450F (230C). Lightly oil a 13 x 9-inch baking pan. Add vegetables to pan and toss with olive oil. Add cumin, oregano, pepper, and salt and toss to coat. Bake 30 minutes or until vegetables are tender. Toss with pasta and serve.

Tangy Chive Pasta with Cucumber Sauce

The secret to this pasta is yogurt, which gives a sour cream flavor with only a fraction of the fat. Make sure to use a natural yogurt. Yogurts with added stabilizers such as gelatin will not work as well. This recipe works well with shorter shapes such as macaroni and penne.

Other recommended accompaniments: Asparagus-Mushroom Sauce (page 131), Creamed Leeks (page 159), Rosy Vegetable Sauce (page 27).

Makes 4 servings.

Tangy Chive Pasta

YIELD: *about 16 ounces*

1 1/4 cups semolina flour
1 1/4 cups all-purpose flour
3 tablespoons minced fresh chives

About 1/2 cup plain nonfat yogurt
1 egg white, lightly beaten

Combine flours in pasta machine bowl. Mix 1 minute, until blended. Add chives and mix 1 minute.

Using a fork, mix 1/2 cup yogurt with egg white until blended. With pasta machine running, slowly add yogurt mixture over a period of 3 minutes, reserving 2 tablespoons. Let machine continue to mix another minute. The dough should consist of lumps the size of peas and walnut halves. If it seems too dry, gradually add reserved yogurt mixture, then more yogurt, 1/2 tablespoon at a time. If it seems too wet, add more semolina flour, 1 tablespoon at a time.

When the dough is the proper consistency, extrude according to the manufacturer's instructions.

When the sauce is ready, cook pasta in boiling water 2 to 6 minutes. Drain pasta and place in a large bowl.

Cucumber Sauce

YIELD: *1 1/2 cups*

1/2 cup plain nonfat yogurt
1 1/2 teaspoons olive oil
1/8 teaspoon salt
1/4 teaspoon freshly ground black
  pepper

1 1/2 cups peeled, seeded, and diced
  cucumbers (1 to 2 cucumbers)
3 tablespoons chopped fresh chives

Combine yogurt, olive oil, salt, pepper, and cucumber. Toss with cooked pasta. Sprinkle with chives and serve.

Pesto Pasta with Pesto

When I was growing up in a very non-Italian neighborhood, pesto was an unknown concept to me. The only Italian sauce was tomato—with or without meat. Then I moved to New England, with its many Italian neighborhoods, and I met pesto. I was immediately seduced by the pungent blend of fresh basil, garlic, olive oil, Parmesan cheese, and pine nuts. It had a touch of the exotic and tasted wonderful. Today, pesto has become almost commonplace, with even large commercial manufacturers producing pestos.

Literally, pesto means "paste," because traditionally the fresh basil and nuts were pounded into a paste with a mortar and pestle. Today, a food-processor simplifies the procedure, and there are many varieties of pesto or pastelike sauces—olive, sun-dried tomato, and every variety of fresh herbs and greens.

Traditional pesto is very rich: For 2 cups of basil leaves there might be as much as 3/4 cup of olive oil. I find this too rich for me, so I have cut back significantly on the oil. I also like a milder garlic flavor, but if you are a garlic fan, by all means, use more garlic! Be sure to wash the basil leaves before using them; they can be gritty.

Note that the recipe makes extra sauce, about twice what you need for the pasta. I like to make extra pesto in the summer, when basil is at its peak, and freeze it. Having frozen pesto on hand gives you a bright taste of summer during the cold winter months.

This recipe works well with the spaghetti and linguine dies.

Other recommended accompaniments: Chunky Tomato Sauce (page 171), Roasted Garlic Sauce and Peas (page 37), Sun-Dried Tomato Pesto (page 23).

Makes 4 servings.

Pesto Pasta

YIELD: *16 ounces*

4 cups packed fresh basil leaves
    (about 2 bunches)
3 cloves garlic, peeled
1 egg

1 tablespoon extra-virgin olive oil
1 1/4 cups semolina flour
1 1/4 cups all-purpose flour
Water, as needed

Place basil leaves in the bowl of a food processor. Turn processor on and drop garlic cloves through the feed tube. Puree until leaves are reduced to a coarse paste. There should be about 1 1/3 cups basil puree. Remove 1/3 cup and set aside remaining puree to use in the pesto below.

Mix the 1/3 cup basil puree with the egg and olive oil. There should be a little more than 1/2 cup.

Combine flours in pasta machine bowl. Mix 1 minute, until blended.

With pasta machine running, slowly add basil mixture over a period of 3 minutes. Let machine continue to mix another minute. The dough should consist of lumps the size of peas and walnut halves. If it seems too dry, gradually add water, 1/2 tablespoon at a time. If it seems too wet, add more semolina flour, 1 tablespoon at a time.

When the dough is the proper consistency, extrude according to the manufacturer's instructions.

When the pesto is ready, cook pasta in boiling water 2 to 6 minutes. Drain pasta and place in a large bowl.

Pesto

YIELD: *1 1/3 cups; 8 servings*

6 tablespoons pine nuts
About 1 cup basil puree (from above)
3 tablespoons extra-virgin olive oil
1/8 teaspoon salt

1/3 cup grated Parmesan cheese
1 tablespoon butter
4 basil leaves, for garnish

Toast the pine nuts: Heat pine nuts in a small, dry, heavy-bottomed skillet over high heat until beginning to brown slightly, about 3 minutes. Reduce heat to medium high and continue to toast, stirring, until most nuts are golden brown or have patches of golden brown. Immediately remove nuts from pan (they will continue to toast otherwise) and let cool for a few minutes. Set aside 2 tablespoons of toasted nuts.

In the bowl of a food processor, combine remaining 4 tablespoons of pine nuts, the basil puree, olive oil, and salt. Puree until blended. Add Parmesan cheese and pulse until incorporated.

Toss drained pasta with butter to coat the pasta thoroughly. When butter has melted over pasta, add 2/3 cup of the pesto and toss to coat. The remaining 2/3 cup pesto can be refrigerated up to 3 days or frozen up to 3 months.

To serve, divide pasta among 4 plates. Sprinkle 1/2 tablespoon pine nuts over each serving and garnish with a basil leaf.

Merlot-Tarragon Pasta with Green Bean–Red Onion Sauce

This recipe works best when the sauce and pasta are made together (although you can make the pasta in advance and store it). Ideally, start the sauce before you begin making the pasta. This will give the onions time to caramelize. The onions absorb the wine and become redder, an attractive contrast to the green of the beans.

Shorter shapes work best with this recipe, such as fusilli, penne, or ziti.

Other recommended accompaniments: Asparagus, Leeks, and Red Peppers (page 33), Chestnut-Mushroom Delight (page 85), Kale, Leeks, and Potatoes (page 79), Roasted Garlic Sauce and Peas (page 37).

Makes 4 servings.

Merlot-Tarragon Pasta

YIELD: *about 16 ounces*

1 1/4 cups semolina flour
1 1/4 cups all-purpose flour
1 tablespoon chopped fresh tarragon
    or 1 teaspoon dried

About 1/2 cup Merlot or other
    full-bodied red wine

Combine flours in pasta machine bowl. Mix 1 minute, until blended. Add tarragon and mix 1 minute.

With pasta machine running, slowly add 1/2 cup Merlot over a period of 3 minutes. Let machine continue to mix another minute. The dough should consist of lumps the size of peas and walnut halves. If it seems too dry, gradually add more wine, 1/2 tablespoon at a time. If it seems too wet, add more semolina flour, 1 tablespoon at a time.

When the dough is the proper consistency, extrude according to the manufacturer's instructions.

When the sauce is almost ready, cook pasta in boiling water 2 to 6 minutes. Drain pasta, reserving 1/2 cup cooking water, and place in a large bowl.

Green Bean–Red Onion Sauce

YIELD: *4 servings*

1 tablespoon olive oil
2 medium red onions, quartered and
    thinly sliced (about 2 cups)
3/4 pound green beans, ends trimmed
    and cut into 1-inch pieces
    (about 3 cups)

1 cup Merlot wine
1/2 teaspoon salt
1/4 teaspoon freshly ground black
    pepper
1/2 cup pasta cooking water

Heat olive oil in a large skillet over medium heat. Add onions and cook, stirring occasionally, about 30 minutes or until they start to brown slightly and caramelize.

Add chopped green beans and cook, stirring, over medium heat about 2 minutes. Add 1/4 cup of the wine and the salt and cook, stirring occasionally, until the liquid has evaporated. Add another 1/2 cup of the wine, partially cover, and cook 5 minutes, until most of the wine has evaporated. Add remaining 1/4 cup wine, stir, and re-cover. Cook 5 minutes or until beans are cooked through, soft yet slightly crunchy. Add pepper and adjust the seasoning to taste.

Add reserved 1/2 cup pasta cooking water to the beans and stir. Add pasta, remove from heat, and stir pasta to mix thoroughly with green bean and red onion mixture. Serve immediately.

Herbes de Provence Pasta with Zucchini Mélange

This pasta is laced with the flavors of the Mediterranean. The wine in the pasta is complemented by the summery vegetables. Herbes de Provence *is an herb mixture made of dried herbs that grow in the Provence region of France. The herb combinations vary, and I've seen some recipes that include basil, fennel, lavender, and dried orange peel. A good gourmet store will sell* herbes de Provence, *or you can check the sources at the end of the book. You can also make your own* herbes de Provence *mixture: Combine 1/2 teaspoon each of dried marjoram, oregano, savory, rosemary, and thyme. Mix together, then use 2 teaspoons of the mixture for the pasta and 1/2 teaspoon for the Zucchini Mélange.*

Zucchini is a vegetable I've always considered bland and uninteresting. But it has a good texture, and when it is combined with herbes de Provence *and capers, the results are delicious. This is a perfect use for surplus zucchini.*

This recipe works well with wider dies such as papardelle or fettuccine.

Other recommended accompaniments: Apple, Leeks, and Brie (page 41), Niçoise Mix (page 99), Tomatoes Fresco (page 67), Walnut–Goat Cheese Sauce (page 35).

Makes 4 to 6 servings.

Herbes de Provence Pasta

YIELD: *about 16 ounces*

1 1/4 cups semolina flour
1 1/4 cups all-purpose flour
2 teaspoons dried *herbes de Provence*

1/2 to 3/4 cup dry white wine

Combine flours in pasta machine bowl. Mix 1 minute, until blended. Add *herbes de Provence* and mix 1 minute.

With pasta machine running, slowly add 1/2 cup wine over a period of 3 minutes. Let machine continue to mix another minute. The dough should consist of lumps the size of peas and walnut halves. If it seems too dry, gradually add more wine, 1/2 tablespoon at a time. If it seems too wet, add more semolina flour, 1 tablespoon at a time.

When the dough is the proper consistency, extrude according to the manufacturer's instructions.

When the zucchini mélange is almost ready, cook pasta in boiling water 2 to 6 minutes. Drain pasta and place in a large bowl.

Zucchini Mélange

YIELD: *3 cups, 4 to 6 servings*

1 tablespoon extra-virgin olive oil	1 summer squash, diced
1 large onion, diced	2 tomatoes, diced
1 clove garlic, minced	2 tablespoons capers
1 medium zucchini, diced	1/2 teaspoon *herbes de Provence*

Heat olive oil in a large skillet over medium-high heat. Add onion and cook, stirring occasionally, until translucent, about 8 to 10 minutes. Stir in garlic and cook 1 minute.

Stir in zucchini and summer squash and cook 2 minutes, then add tomatoes. Cook, uncovered, over medium-high heat, until liquids begin to boil. Reduce heat and simmer 10 minutes.

Stir in capers and *herbes de Provence* and cook 2 to 3 minutes. Spoon over pasta, toss to combine, and serve immediately.

Cilantro Pasta with Cilantro-Lime Pesto

Cilantro, also called coriander, looks a lot like parsley but has a very different flavor, and its seeds are dried and ground to produce the spice coriander. It is a distinctive herb with an intriguing, slightly lemony flavor that can be found in several ethnic cuisines, including South American, Mediterranean, and Indian. In this recipe cilantro is combined with lime juice and pumpkin seeds (available in natural food and Hispanic markets), which gives it a Mexican flair.

This recipe works well with the spaghetti and linguine dies. The pesto recipe makes twice the amount you need, but I like to make extra and then have the sauce on hand. It also makes a tasty spread.

Other recommended accompaniments: Curried Lentil Soup (page 29), Watercress, Fresh Mozzarella, and Lime Vinaigrette (page 45), Roasted Tomato and Corn Salsa (page 77), Spicy Cheddar Sauce (page 143).

Makes 4 servings.

Cilantro Pasta

YIELD: *16 ounces*

1 1/4 cups semolina flour
1 1/4 cups all-purpose flour
1/2 cup plus 2 tablespoons packed
 fresh cilantro leaves, coarsely
 chopped

Grated zest of 1 lime
5 tablespoons fresh lime juice
About 1/4 cup water

Combine flours in pasta machine bowl. Mix 1 minute, until blended. Add cilantro and lime zest and mix 1 minute.

Mix together lime juice and 1/4 cup water. With pasta machine running, slowly add juice mixture over a period of 3 minutes, reserving 2 tablespoons. Let machine continue to mix another minute. The dough should consist of lumps the size of peas and walnut halves. If it seems too dry, gradually add reserved juice mixture, then water, 1/2 tablespoon at a time. If it seems too wet, add more semolina flour, 1 tablespoon at a time.

When the dough is the proper consistency, extrude according to the manufacturer's instructions.

When the pesto is ready, cook pasta in boiling water 2 to 6 minutes. Drain pasta and place in a large bowl.

Cilantro-Lime Pesto

YIELD: *3/4 cup*

3 tablespoons shelled pumpkin seeds
2 cups packed fresh cilantro leaves
    (about 2 bunches, thick stems
    removed)
2 small cloves garlic, peeled

1 ounce Romano cheese, cut into
    1/4-inch chunks
1/4 cup extra-virgin olive oil
3 tablespoons fresh lime juice
1/2 teaspoon salt

Toast the pumpkin seeds: Add seeds to a small, dry, heavy-bottomed skillet over medium-high heat. They may pop as they begin to heat up. Heat 3 to 4 minutes or until slightly puffed and pale brown in spots. Or, place seeds on a microwave-safe glass plate and cook on HIGH 4 minutes. Set toasted seeds aside to cool slightly.

Place cilantro in the bowl of a food processor fitted with the steel blade. Pulse a few times to chop finely. With machine running, add garlic, then pumpkin seeds, then cubes of Romano cheese through feed tube.

Stop food processor and scrape down the sides of the bowl. Drizzle in oil and lime juice and sprinkle with salt. Puree until blended, stopping to scrape down sides of the bowl once or twice.

To serve, toss half of the pesto with the cooked pasta.

The remaining pesto will keep in the refrigerator up to 3 days, and in the freezer up to 3 months.

Horseradish Pasta with Smoked Trout Sauce

Smoked trout is a delicately flavored smoked fish, slightly less assertive than smoked salmon but distinctive nonetheless. I always order it when restaurants have it on the menu. It is generally served with a horseradish–sour cream sauce, capers, red onions, finely chopped or grated hard-cooked egg, and toast points. I put these flavor favorites together for this zingy horseradish pasta. I prefer to use white horseradish, although pink may be used—it will slightly color the pasta. Smoked salmon may be substituted for the trout.

This is a cold pasta dish, good as an appetizer and lunch entrée. I like to make this pasta with the papardelle or fettuccine dies, cutting it into 3- to 4-inch lengths.

Other recommended accompaniments: Creamed Leeks (page 159), Mustard Vinaigrette and Corned Beef (page 89), Walnut–Goat Cheese Sauce (page 35).

Makes 4 entrées or 6 appetizers.

Horseradish Pasta

YIELD: *16 ounces*

1 1/4 cups semolina flour
1 1/4 cups all-purpose flour
1 egg

1 tablespoon prepared horseradish
1/3 to 1/2 cup plain yogurt

Combine flours in pasta machine bowl. Mix 1 minute, until blended.

Lightly beat egg in a measuring cup. Stir in horseradish and add enough yogurt to make 2/3 cup liquid.

With pasta machine running, slowly add yogurt mixture over a period of 3 minutes, reserving 2 tablespoons. Let machine continue to mix another minute. The dough should consist of lumps the size of peas and walnut halves. If it seems too dry, gradually add reserved yogurt mixture, then more yogurt, 1/2 tablespoon at a time. If it seems too wet, add more semolina flour, 1 tablespoon at a time.

When the dough is the proper consistency, extrude according to the manufacturer's instructions.

When sauce is ready, cook pasta in boiling water 2 to 6 minutes. Drain pasta.

Smoked Trout Sauce

YIELD: *4 entrées or 6 appetizers*

1 slice whole-wheat bread
2 teaspoons butter
1/4 cup plain yogurt
1/4 cup sour cream
1/4 teaspoon freshly ground black
    pepper
1/8 teaspoon salt

1/2 smoked trout fillet (about
    8 ounces), boned and cut into
    1/4- to 1/2-inch pieces
2 tablespoons capers
1 hard-cooked egg, grated
2 tablespoons minced red onion

Lightly toast bread. Spread 1 teaspoon butter on each side of toast. Cut toast into 1/4-inch squares and brown them slightly in a small skillet over medium-high heat. When they are golden brown, remove and set croutons aside.

Whisk together yogurt, sour cream, pepper, and salt. Rinse drained pasta with cold water until cool, then drain again. Put pasta into a large bowl and toss to coat with the yogurt mixture. Add smoked trout pieces, capers, grated egg, and minced onion and toss to combine.

To serve, place pasta on individual plates and garnish with a few croutons. Serve at room temperature or chilled.

Fresh Ginger Pasta with Stir-Fried Vegetables

Chinese dishes are most commonly served over rice, but there are also several dishes that use Chinese egg noodles. These are egg noodles with a twist—freshly grated ginger.

Fresh ginger imparts a wonderful spiciness to this pasta. I find that the best way to grate fresh ginger is with a food processor. Peel the ginger root and cut into 1-inch chunks. With the machine running, using the steel blade, drop in the chunks through the feed tube. The ginger will be finely minced. I like to prepare large quantities and then freeze it.

I recommend cutting the pasta into linguine or fettuccine.

Other recommended accompaniments: American Turkey Fessenjen (page 113), Coconut-Squash Sauce (page 31), Mango Chutney Sauce (page 161).

Makes 6 servings.

Fresh Ginger Pasta

YIELD: *about 16 ounces*

1 1/4 cups semolina flour
1 1/4 cups all-purpose flour
3 tablespoons grated ginger root

2 eggs, lightly beaten
Water, as needed

Combine flours in pasta machine bowl. Mix 1 minute, until blended. Add ginger and mix 1 minute.

With pasta machine running, slowly add beaten eggs over a period of 3 minutes. Let machine continue to mix another minute. The dough should consist of lumps the size of peas and walnut halves. If it seems too dry, gradually add water, 1/2 tablespoon at a time. If it seems too wet, add more semolina flour, 1 tablespoon at a time.

When the dough is the proper consistency, extrude according to the manufacturer's instructions.

When the vegetables are almost ready, cook pasta in boiling water 2 to 6 minutes. Drain pasta and place in a large bowl.

Stir-Fried Vegetables

YIELD: *6 servings*

1 ounce dried shiitake mushrooms
1 cup boiling water
2 teaspoons cornstarch
3 tablespoons soy sauce
2 tablespoons toasted sesame oil
1 tablespoon rice vinegar
2 teaspoons honey
2 tablespoons minced or grated
    ginger root
1 pound extra-firm tofu, cut into
    1/2-inch cubes
1 tablespoon peanut oil

1 bunch green onions, white and
    green parts, thinly sliced
1 green bell pepper, cut into 1/2-
    inch pieces
1 red bell pepper, cut into 1/2-inch
    pieces
1 (8-ounce) can water chestnuts,
    drained and cut into 1/8-inch
    slices
1 (15-ounce) can baby corn,
    drained and rinsed
1 cup mung bean sprouts

Pour boiling water over shiitake mushrooms in a bowl. Cover and set aside 15 to 20 minutes, until mushrooms are softened. Or, pour 1 cup water over mushrooms in a microwave-safe bowl. Cover with plastic wrap and cook on HIGH 4 minutes. Let stand, covered, 4 minutes, then proceed.

Remove mushrooms from liquid, squeezing slightly to squeeze out extra liquid. Cut each mushroom into 4 to 5 slices and set aside. Reserve 1/2 cup of the soaking liquid, making sure not to get any of the grit that might be at the bottom. Remove 1 tablespoon of the reserved liquid and mix it with the cornstarch until smooth. Gradually stir in remaining liquid and 1 tablespoon of the soy sauce and set this mixture aside.

While mushrooms are soaking, combine remaining 2 tablespoons soy sauce, 1 tablespoon of the sesame oil, the rice vinegar, honey, and 1 tablespoon of the ginger. Pour over tofu cubes in a small bowl, stir gently to coat the tofu completely, and marinate the tofu about 20 minutes.

Heat a wok or large skillet over high heat. Add peanut oil and remaining 1 tablespoon sesame oil and swirl it around the pan. When a drop of water splatters off the surface, add green onions and remaining 1 tablespoon ginger. Cook, stirring, 1 minute, then add bell peppers. Cook, stirring, 1 minute, then stir in water chestnuts, baby corn, and tofu with marinade. Add the bean sprouts.

Stir cornstarch mixture and pour over vegetables. Cook, stirring, until vegetables are glazed, about 3 minutes.

Add drained pasta and stir to mix thoroughly with the vegetables. Serve immediately.

Fennel Pasta with Fresh Fennel–Anchovy Sauté

Fennel has a unique slightly sweet, slightly savory flavor reminiscent of licorice (but much better, in my opinion). Its flavor is similar to that of anise, but much milder and less sweet. The anchovies add a salty, briny touch to the dish. Fresh fennel, which is sometimes called anise, is a round white bulb, about 4 to 5 inches across, usually sold with stems and feathery dill-like leaves attached. This recipe works well with any die.

Other recommended accompaniments: Chunky Tomato Sauce (page 171), Creamed Leeks (page 159), Apple, Leeks, and Brie (page 41), Vegetable Soup (page 173).

Makes 4 servings.

Fennel Pasta

YIELD: *16 ounces*

1 1/4 cups semolina flour
1 1/4 cups all-purpose flour
2 teaspoons crushed fennel seeds

1/2 to 2/3 cup water
1 tablespoon extra-virgin olive oil

Combine flours in pasta machine bowl. Mix 1 minute, until blended. Add fennel seeds and mix 1 minute.

Combine 1/2 cup water and olive oil. With pasta machine running, slowly add oil mixture over a period of 3 minutes. Let machine continue to mix another minute. The dough should consist of lumps the size of peas and walnut halves. If it seems too dry, gradually add more water, 1/2 tablespoon at a time. If it seems too wet, add more semolina flour, 1 tablespoon at a time.

When the dough is the proper consistency, extrude according to the manufacturer's instructions.

When the sauce is almost ready, cook pasta in boiling water 2 to 6 minutes. Drain pasta and place in a large bowl.

Fresh Fennel–Anchovy Sauté

YIELD: *4 servings*

1 tablespoon extra-virgin olive oil
1 bunch green onions, white and
    most of green parts, thinly sliced
1 large bulb fresh fennel, stems and
    base removed, quartered and
    thinly sliced

1 stalk celery, thinly sliced
6 anchovies
1 tablespoon tomato paste
1/2 cup red wine
2 tablespoons currants (optional)
1 tablespoon butter

Heat olive oil in large saucepan over medium-high heat. Add green onions, reserving 1/4 cup of sliced greens to add later. Add fennel and celery and cook over medium heat 3 minutes.

Add anchovies, pressing anchovies with back of a spoon to break them up. They should mash into a kind of paste. Stir to combine.

Mix tomato paste with 1 tablespoon of red wine until smooth. Gradually stir in remaining wine, making sure to keep the mixture smooth. Add wine mixture to fennel and stir to mix. Bring to a boil, then reduce heat to medium. Add currants, if using. Cover and cook over medium heat about 10 minutes, until fennel is almost tender and can be pierced easily with a fork.

Uncover and stir in butter until melted, making sure it is mixed with other ingredients. Toss with pasta and serve immediately.

Black Pepper Pasta with Tomatoes Fresco

Black pepper gives this pasta a spicy punch; if your palate is less tolerant, use less pepper. A touch of white wine in the pasta marries well with the pepper, and both are complemented by the fresh tomatoes in the sauce. This is a good pasta to make in the summertime, when tomatoes are at their most abundant and most flavorful. This recipe works well with any die.

Other recommended accompaniments: Beef 'n' Beer Goulash (page 115), Chunky Tomato Sauce (page 171), Puttanesca Sauce (page 139), Zucchini Mélange (page 57).

Makes 4 servings.

Black Pepper Pasta

YIELD: *16 ounces*

1 1/4 cups semolina flour
1 1/4 cups all-purpose flour
1 teaspoon freshly ground black
    pepper

2 large eggs
1/4 cup white wine

Combine flours in pasta machine bowl. Mix 1 minute, until blended.

Lightly beat eggs together with the white wine.

With pasta machine running, slowly add 1/2 cup of the egg mixture over a period of 3 minutes. Let machine continue to mix another minute. The dough should consist of lumps the size of peas and walnut halves. If it seems too dry, gradually add more egg mixture, 1/2 tablespoon at a time. If it seems too wet, add more semolina flour, 1 tablespoon at a time.

When the dough is the proper consistency, extrude according to the manufacturer's instructions.

When the sauce is almost ready, cook pasta in boiling water 2 to 6 minutes. Drain pasta and place in a large bowl.

Tomatoes Fresco

YIELD: *4 servings*

2 large tomatoes
2 tablespoons minced chives
1/8 to 1 teaspoon sugar

1/8 teaspoon salt
1 tablespoon extra-virgin olive oil

Peel tomatoes: Drop tomatoes into boiling water for 1 minute. Remove immediately and rinse under cold running water. The skins should slip off easily.

Cut tomatoes in half and scoop out the seeds into a bowl to catch all the juices. Strain the juices and seeds through a strainer; discard seeds. Dice tomatoes and toss with chives, 1/8 teaspoon sugar, and salt. Add juice and taste. If mixture is particularly acidic, add more sugar. It should taste smooth, not noticeably sweet, but not too acidic.

Toss drained pasta with olive oil. Pour tomato mixture over pasta, toss, and serve immediately.

Chocolate Mole Pasta with Chicken Mole Sauce

I've seen two etymological roots cited for the word mole: *the Spanish* moler, *"to grind," and the Aztec* molli, *which means "concoction." Both meanings describe this exotic Mexican dish, a concoction of several ingredients ground together to form a smooth sauce. These ingredients usually include nuts, seeds, chiles, several spices, and, often, a secret ingredient—unsweetened chocolate. The sauce takes time to prepare and should be made before the pasta.*

This recipe calls for 1/2 ounce unsweetened chocolate. For a richer chocolate flavor, increase the amount to 1 ounce. The sauce is mildly spiced with chile flakes; if you like hotter sauces, increase the amount. This recipes works well with the papardelle, fettuccine, and linguine dies.

Other recommended accompaniments: Coconut-Squash Sauce (page 31), Garlicky Chile con Carne (page 120), Orange Butter Sauce (page 43), Rosy Vegetable Sauce (page 27).

Makes 6 servings.

Chocolate Mole Pasta

YIELD: *16 ounces*

1 1/4 cups semolina flour
1 1/4 cups all-purpose flour
2 tablespoons unsweetened cocoa
    powder
1/2 teaspoon ground dried chile
1/2 teaspoon ground coriander

1/8 teaspoon ground cloves
4 teaspoons toasted sesame seeds
    (see Note, below)
1/2 to 3/4 cup vegetable stock or
    cooled chicken cooking liquid
    (opposite)

Combine flours, cocoa, chile powder, coriander, cloves, and toasted sesame seeds in pasta machine bowl. Mix 1 minute, until blended.

With pasta machine running, slowly add 1/2 cup stock over a period of 3 minutes. Let machine continue to mix another minute. The dough should consist of lumps the size of peas and walnut halves. If it seems too dry, gradually add more stock, 1/2 tablespoon at a time. If it seems too wet, add more semolina flour, 1 tablespoon at a time.

When the dough is the proper consistency, extrude according to the manufacturer's instructions. When the sauce is ready, cook pasta in boiling water 2 to 6 minutes. Drain pasta and place in a large bowl.

Chicken Mole Sauce

YIELD: *2 1/2 cups sauce*

2 medium boneless, skinless
    chicken breasts
3 cups chicken broth
1/2 cup chopped fresh or canned
    tomatoes
1/2 teaspoon dried chile flakes or to
    taste
1 small onion, diced
1 small clove garlic, minced
1/4 cup raisins plus additional for
    garnish
1 1/2 cups poaching liquid from the
    chicken, or vegetable stock

1/2 cup pine nuts plus additional
    for garnish
1 tablespoon toasted sesame seeds
    (see Note, page 75)
1/4 teaspoon ground cinnamon
1/8 teaspoon ground cloves
1/4 teaspoon ground coriander
1/4 teaspoon anise seeds
1/2 teaspoon salt
2 teaspoons corn oil
1/2 ounce unsweetened chocolate

Cut each chicken breast in half. Place chicken in a medium saucepan, cover with broth, and bring to a boil. Reduce heat and simmer gently 12 to 15 minutes or until chicken is cooked through. Remove chicken and let cool slightly, then cut into 1/2-inch chunks. Set aside. Reserve the chicken poaching liquid to use in the sauce.

Place tomatoes, chile flakes, onion, garlic, and raisins and 1 cup of the reserved chicken cooking liquid in a large skillet. Simmer 20 minutes or until onion is softened.

Add pine nuts and sesame seeds to a blender or food processor and pulse to grind into a powder. Add cinnamon, cloves, coriander, anise, and salt and pulse to blend. Add tomato mixture and blend 1 to 2 minutes or until all the ingredients are pureed into a smooth sauce.

Heat corn oil in a large skillet over medium-high heat. Add sauce from the blender and the unsweetened chocolate. Cook, stirring, until chocolate has melted. Add chicken to the sauce and cook over low heat, stirring occasionally, until heated through, about 10 minutes.

To serve, divide pasta onto 6 plates and ladle chicken and sauce over each plate. Garnish with a few pine nuts and raisins.

Curried Pasta with Indian Braised Potatoes

Curry powder is generally associated with Indian flavors, but the commercial spice mix hardly does this ancient cuisine justice. The spice mixture actually used for what we think of as curried dishes is called garam masala. *Every region in India has their own garam masala recipe, which consists of a mix of whole spices—anywhere from four or five to over a dozen—that are toasted together and ground. For simplicity's sake, I offer a combination of popular garam masala spices. If you live near an Indian market, you can purchase garam masala, or you may use a good-quality curry powder.*

This recipe works well with any die.

Other recommended accompaniments: American Turkey Fessenjen (page 113), Curried Lentil Soup (page 29), Pumpkin-Cider Sauce (page 135), Sherried Apples and Pecans (page 169).

Makes 6 servings.

Curried Pasta

YIELD: *16 ounces*

1 1/4 cups semolina flour
1 1/4 cups all-purpose flour
1 tablespoon garam masala or curry
    powder or 1/2 teaspoon *each*
    ground cinnamon, ground
    cardamom, ground coriander,
    and ground cumin; 1/4 teaspoon
    each ground black pepper and
    ground nutmeg; and 1/8 teaspoon
    each ground cloves and cayenne
    pepper

1/8 teaspoon salt
3 eggs, lightly beaten together
Water, as needed

Combine flours in pasta machine bowl. Mix 1 minute, until blended. Add spices and mix 1 minute.

With pasta machine running, slowly add eggs, reserving about 2 tablespoons, over a period of 3 minutes. Let machine continue to mix another minute. The dough should consist of lumps the size of peas and walnut halves. If it seems too dry, gradually add more egg, then water, 1/2 tablespoon at a time. If it seems too wet, add more semolina flour, 1 tablespoon at a time.

When the dough is the proper consistency, extrude according to the manufacturer's instructions.

When the potatoes are almost ready, cook pasta in boiling water 2 to 6 minutes. Drain pasta.

Indian Braised Potatoes

YIELD: *6 servings*

2 tablespoons unsalted butter
1 tablespoon vegetable oil
1 small onion, minced
1 jalapeño chile (optional), seeded
    and minced
1 1/2 teaspoons cumin seeds
2 tablespoons grated ginger root
1 teaspoon turmeric
4 teaspoons ground coriander

6 large new potatoes (about
    2 pounds), peeled and cut into
    1/2-inch chunks
2 cups water
3/4 teaspoon salt
1 cup chopped fresh spinach
1/4 cup chopped fresh cilantro
1 tablespoon fresh lemon juice

Heat butter and oil in a large skillet over medium heat. Add onion and jalapeño chile, if using, and cook until onion begins to soften, about 4 minutes. Add cumin seeds and ginger and cook 1 minute. Add turmeric and coriander and stir to coat onions. Add potato chunks and stir to coat potatoes with spice mixture. Cook over medium heat 3 to 4 minutes to allow the potatoes to absorb the flavor of the spices.

Add 1 1/2 cups of the water and increase heat to high. Bring to a boil, then reduce heat and simmer. Partially cover and simmer about 10 minutes or until potatoes are tender when pierced with a fork but hold their shape and liquid around the potatoes is reduced and thickened.

Add remaining 1/2 cup water and salt and stir to combine. Add spinach and cook over medium heat 2 to 3 minutes or until spinach is wilted. Stir in cilantro, lemon juice, and drained pasta and serve immediately.

Amber Waves of Grain

Pasta consists of two main parts: dry ingredients, primarily flour, and wet ingredients, such as eggs, vegetable purees, and so on. The easiest way to vary the final pasta results is with wet ingredients, as demonstrated in other chapters. But the type of flour used can affect the results as well, and in this chapter I offer several pastas made with a variety of grains.

Some of these grains are readily available at the supermarket; for others you may need to go to a specialty or natural food store, or order them from one of the mail-order sources at the back of the book.

Flour made from nonwheat grains, such as corn, buckwheat, and rice, tends to have little or no gluten, and gluten is what helps the pasta hold its shape well. Therefore, pasta made using flour from these other grains works best when mixed with wheat flour. Many of these doughs are more delicate than all-wheat flour doughs. For this reason, I found that I preferred using eggs as a liquid, because of the binding qualities of the albumin in the egg white. Some recipes do still work with water, and there are a few egg-free recipes as well.

Whole-Wheat Pasta with Spicy Peanut Sauce

One of my favorite sauces for noodles is an Asian peanut-sesame sauce. These are sometimes called dan-dan *noodles (with various transliterated spellings) in Chinese restaurants. The sauce goes particularly well with whole-wheat pasta, which has its own nutty flavor.*

Initially, I tried to incorporate some of the sauce into the pasta itself. This was when I discovered that too much fat in the pasta mix makes the pasta dissolve when you try to cook it. Sesame oil in particular does not seem to yield pasta with a good texture when cooked. The sauce will keep in the refrigerator for about a week.

I recommend using the linguine or spaghetti die for the noodles.

Other recommended accompaniments: Beef 'n' Beer Goulash (page 115), Gorgonzola Sauce (page 155), Rosy Vegetable Sauce (page 27), Mushroom-Herb Pesto (page 39).

Makes 6 servings.

Whole-Wheat Pasta

YIELD: *16 ounces*

2 1/2 cups whole-wheat flour   Water, as needed
3 large eggs, lightly beaten together

Add flours to pasta machine bowl. Mix 1 minute, until blended.

With pasta machine running, slowly add eggs over a period of 3 minutes. Let machine continue to mix another minute. The dough should consist of lumps the size of peas and walnut halves. If it seems too dry, gradually add water, 1/2 tablespoon at a time. If it seems too wet, add more flour, 1 tablespoon at a time.

When the dough is the proper consistency, extrude according to the manufacturer's instructions.

When the sauce is almost ready, cook pasta in boiling water 5 to 7 minutes. Drain pasta and place in a large bowl.

Spicy Peanut Sauce

YIELD: *about 3/4 cup*

6 tablespoons peanut butter
    (preferably all-natural, unsalted)
1/4 cup plus 1 tablespoon water
1 tablespoon soy sauce
1 tablespoon rice vinegar or cider
    vinegar
1 tablespoon grated ginger root or
    2 teaspoons ground ginger

1/2 tablespoon honey
1/2 tablespoon fresh lemon juice
Pinch of cayenne pepper
1 tablespoon sesame seeds, toasted
    (see Note, below)
1 to 2 green onions, both white and
    green parts, thinly sliced

Combine peanut butter, water, soy sauce, vinegar, ginger, honey, lemon juice, and cayenne in a blender or food processor and blend until smooth, about 1 minute.

Add sesame seeds to peanut butter mixture, pulsing quickly to mix but not pulverize the seeds.

Add about half the sauce to the cooked pasta and mix to coat noodles. To serve, divide pasta onto 4 plates and sprinkle with sliced green onions. Pass additional sauce on the side.

Note To toast sesame seeds, heat in a small, dry, heavy-bottomed skillet over medium-high heat or until they begin to brown slightly, about 3 minutes. Reduce heat to medium and continue to toast, stirring the seeds, until most are pale gold. Immediately remove seeds from skillet (they will continue to toast otherwise) and let cool for a few minutes.

Chips 'n' Salsa Pasta with Roasted Tomato and Corn Salsa

The winning combination of cornmeal and spiced tomatoes are classic Mexican flavors. The sauce tastes best made with summer's fresh tomatoes and corn taken from the cob, but it also is good made with frozen corn and drained canned tomatoes. I like making this pasta with wide dies such as lasagne or papardelle, cut into 1- to 2-inch lengths.

Other recommended accompaniments: Maquechou (page 83), Chicken Mole Sauce (page 69), Spicy Cheddar Sauce (page 143).

Males 3 to 4 servings.

Chips 'n' Salsa Pasta

YIELD: *12 ounces*

1 cup semolina flour
1/3 cup all-purpose flour
2/3 cup cornmeal
3 tablespoons fresh minced cilantro

About 1/2 cup diced canned tomatoes and chiles
1 large egg white
Water, if needed

Combine flours and cornmeal in pasta machine bowl. Mix 1 minute, until blended. Add minced cilantro and mix 1 minute, until evenly distributed.

Combine tomatoes and chiles and egg white in a blender or food processor and blend until smooth, about 45 seconds.

With pasta machine running, slowly add tomato mixture over a period of 3 minutes, reserving 2 tablespoons. It will be lumpy, and, depending on your machine, you may need a spatula to help it go through the liquid slot on the lid. Let machine continue to mix another minute. The dough should consist of lumps the size of peas and walnut halves. If it seems too dry, gradually add more tomato mixture, then water, 1/2 tablespoon at a time. If it seems too wet, add more semolina flour, 1 tablespoon at a time.

When the dough is the proper consistency, extrude according to the manufacturer's instructions.

When the salsa is ready, cook pasta in boiling water 2 to 6 minutes. Drain pasta and place in a large bowl.

Roasted Tomato and Corn Salsa

YIELD: *3 cups*

1 tablespoon olive oil
1 cup fresh or frozen whole-kernel
    corn
6 green onions, white and some
    green parts, chopped
3 large fresh tomatoes, peeled and
    chopped (see Note, below)

1/8 teaspoon salt
1/4 teaspoon freshly ground pepper
3 tablespoons finely chopped fresh
    cilantro

Preheat oven to 450F (230C). Coat a 13 x 9-inch baking pan with the olive oil.

Add corn, green onions, and tomatoes to pan. Stir to coat with oil. Sprinkle with salt and pepper and stir to combine.

Bake vegetables 30 minutes, or until onions are soft, stirring after 15 minutes.

Remove from oven and stir in chopped cilantro. Toss with pasta. The salsa may be stored up to 3 days in the refrigerator.

Note To peel tomatoes, drop into boiling water for 1 minute. Remove immediately and rinse under cold running water. The skins should slip off easily.

Buckwheat Pasta Baked with Kale, Leeks, and Potatoes (*Pizzochieri*)

Michelle Topor, who leads tours of Boston's North End and teaches Italian cooking classes, mentioned the Italian recipe pizzochieri *to me as a wonderful traditional use of buckwheat pasta in Italy, and I was immediately tempted to make it. This recipe was adapted from one in Marcella Hazan's* Essentials of Classic Italian Cooking *(Knopf, 1992). It is a hearty winter dish, rich, delicious, and addictive. Other greens may be substituted for the kale; Hazan uses just the stems of Swiss chard. I've seen other recipes using both stems and leaves of chard, or Savoy cabbage. Topor says it works well with any greens. I chose kale because it was in season at my local farmers' market, and it is extremely nutritious.*

I recommend using the fettuccine die, cutting off the pasta at about 4-inch lengths.

Other recommended accompaniments: Poached Salmon and Spinach Beurre Blanc (page 101), Roasted Peppers and Herbs (page 141), Mushroom-Herb Pesto (page 39), Sole Amandine (page 105).

Makes 6 servings.

Buckwheat Pasta

YIELD: *about 16 ounces*

1 cup buckwheat flour
1 1/2 cups all-purpose flour

3 large eggs
Milk, as needed

Combine flours in pasta machine bowl. Mix 1 minute, until blended.

Beat eggs in a 2-cup measuring cup. Add enough milk to make 3/4 cup of liquid and mix well with eggs.

With the pasta machine running, slowly add most of the egg mixture over a period of 3 minutes, reserving 2 to 3 tablespoons. Let machine continue to mix another minute. The dough should consist of lumps the size of peas and walnut halves. If it seems too dry, gradually add remaining egg mixture, 1/2 tablespoon at a time. If it seems too wet, add more all-purpose flour, 1 tablespoon at a time.

When the dough is the proper consistency, extrude according to the manufacturer's instructions.

If using the pasta with the Kale, Leeks, and Potatoes, set it aside, uncooked and loosely covered with plastic wrap, while you prepare the kale mixture, or cook pasta in boiling water 2 to 6 minutes to use in other recipes.

Kale, Leeks, and Potatoes

YIELD: *6 servings*

1 tablespoon unsalted butter
1 tablespoon extra-virgin olive oil
3 cloves garlic, peeled and sliced
3 leaves fresh sage or 1/4 teaspoon
    dried sage
2 cups thinly sliced leeks, white and
    pale green parts (about 2 leeks),
    rinsed well
6 kale leaves

2 large new or Red Bliss potatoes,
    peeled and cut into 1/4-inch
    slices
8 quarts water
2 tablespoons salt
1 cup grated Fontina cheese,
    preferably Italian Fontina
1/2 cup grated Parmesan cheese

Preheat oven to 400F (205C). Butter a 13 x 9-inch baking dish; set aside.

Heat butter and olive oil in a medium skillet over medium heat. Add garlic and cook until it begins to brown. Using a fork or slotted spoon, remove garlic slices from the skillet and discard. Add sage to the butter and oil remaining in skillet and cook, stirring, about 30 seconds, then add leeks. Cook leeks over medium-low heat until soft, about 15 minutes.

Meanwhile, bring water and salt to a boil in a large stockpot. Remove kale stems from leaves and chop into 1/4-inch slices. Coarsely chop the leaves. Add kale stems to boiling water and cook 2 minutes, then add kale leaves. Cook 8 minutes, then add potato slices. Cook until kale and potatoes are tender, about 7 to 10 minutes.

Add the pasta and cook until just barely tender to the bite, about 1 minute if the pasta is fresh, 2 minutes if it has been refrigerated. Drain well immediately and pour pasta, kale, and potatoes into buttered baking dish; set aside.

Pour cooked leeks on top of the pasta mixture and mix to combine. Add Fontina and Parmesan cheeses and stir to combine. Smooth the top of the mixture and place in preheated oven. Bake 10 minutes or until cheeses are melted. Remove from oven, let stand about 3 minutes, then serve.

Asian Buckwheat Pasta in Miso Broth with Wasabi Drizzle

Buckwheat noodles found in Asian markets and health food stores are generally made with water as the liquid, as opposed to eggs, as in the Italian-inspired recipe above. In Japan, buckwheat noodles are called soba, *and are served hot in broths and soups, or cold with dipping sauces.*

For this recipe the noodles are served in a simple-to-make miso broth. Miso, a savory paste made from fermented soybeans, is the base for many Japanese soups. It is very healthful, like a vegetarian chicken soup. The miso paste is available in Asian markets and in natural food stores, and comes in a few varieties. Mellow white miso is actually pale gold, and has a milder flavor. Red miso is brownish red and has a stronger flavor. The miso paste is simply mixed with water, and, voilà, broth.

I recommend using the linguine or spaghetti die, cutting off the pasta at about 8-inch lengths.

Other recommended accompaniments: Pad Thai (page 91), Roasted Garlic Sauce and Peas (page 37), Spicy Peanut Sauce (page 75), Stir-Fried Vegetables (page 63).

Makes 6 servings.

Asian Buckwheat Pasta

YIELD: *about 16 ounces*

1 cup buckwheat flour
1 1/2 cups whole-wheat flour

1/2 teaspoon salt
1/2 to 3/4 cup water

Combine flours in pasta machine bowl. Mix 1 minute, until blended.

Dissolve salt in 1/2 cup water. With pasta machine running, slowly add most of the salted water over a period of 3 minutes. Let machine continue to mix another minute. The dough should consist of lumps the size of peas and walnut halves. If it seems too dry, gradually add more water, 1/2 tablespoon at a time. If it seems too wet, add more wheat flour, 1 tablespoon at a time.

When the dough is the proper consistency, extrude according to the manufacturer's instructions.

Add pasta to boiling salted water and stir. When water returns to a boil, add 1 cup cold water. When the water returns to a boil, you have two options: If you are using the noodles for the miso broth, cook the noodles 1 more minute, then drain and immediately rinse with cold water until the noodles are cold. Set aside until the soup is ready.

If you are cooking the noodles to eat plain or with a sauce, add another 1 cup cold water and let the water return to a boil. Immediately test a noodle; it should be just tender to the bite. If too firm, check again after 1 minute. Drain noodles and immediately rinse with cold water. If you are serving them cold, mix with the sauce of your choice. If you are serving them hot, pour boiling water over the noodles just before serving.

Miso Broth with Wasabi Drizzle

YIELD: *6 servings*

10 cups water
5 green onions, white and green parts,
    thinly sliced
2 kale leaves, stems removed,
    chopped
1/2 cup plus 1 tablespoon red miso
8 ounces firm tofu, cut into 1/2-inch
    cubes

1 recipe Asian Buckwheat Pasta
    (cooked as directed)
12 snow pea pods

WASABI DRIZZLE
2 teaspoons wasabi powder
2 teaspoons water
3 tablespoons soy sauce

In a large pot, bring water to a boil. Set aside some of the sliced green onions to use as garnish. Add kale and remaining green onions and boil 10 minutes, until kale is tender. Reduce heat to a simmer.

Add miso paste to a bowl. Add about 1/2 cup of the simmering water and mix until smooth. Add another 1/2 cup water and mix. Continue adding water until mixture is the consistency of heavy cream. Pour the miso mixture into the simmering kale mixture and stir to combine. Add tofu and noodles to water and increase heat so mixture comes to a slow boil. Cook 2 or 3 minutes or until noodles are just tender to the bite. Add the snow peas and cook 1 minute.

Prepare Wasabi Drizzle: Combine wasabi powder and water and mix to make a thick paste. Add soy sauce 1 tablespoon at a time and mix thoroughly. Serve soup in deep bowls, drizzled with 1 teaspoon of Wasabi Drizzle and garnished with reserved green onions.

Toasted Amaranth Pasta with Maquechou

Amaranth is an ancient grain that is very high in protein. It has a distinctive flavor that is mellowed by toasting. This is flavorful pasta; it even tastes good plain. Corn, another ancient grain, enhances the flavor. Both toasted and regular amaranth flour can be found in natural food stores, or ordered by mail (see "Sources," pages 197–198).

Maquechou is an African-American dish from southern Louisiana. While they agree on the basic ingredients, different cooks favor various proportions and preparations. Some advocate a long cooking, up to a couple of hours, which yields a thick, soft stew. The recipe below is a speedier preparation. It is especially tasty made with fresh corn off the cob; I like the slight, juicy crunch the kernels maintain. Frozen corn may be used instead, but fresh corn imparts a superior flavor to the dish. This recipe was inspired by one in The Welcome Table: African American Heritage Cooking *by Jessica B. Harris (Simon & Schuster, 1995).*

I like making this pasta with fettuccine or papardelle dies, cut into 4- to 5-inch lengths.

Other recommended accompaniments: American Turkey Fessenjen (page 113), Apple, Leeks, and Brie (page 41), Sun-Dried Tomato Pesto (page 23), Sweet-and-Sour Sardines (page 103).

Makes 4 servings.

Toasted Amaranth Pasta

YIELD: *12 ounces*

1/2 cup semolina flour
1/2 cup all-purpose flour
1 cup toasted amaranth flour

2 large eggs, lightly beaten together
Water, as needed

Combine flours in pasta machine bowl. Mix 1 minute, until blended.

With pasta machine running, slowly add eggs over a period of 3 minutes. Let machine continue to mix another minute. The dough should consist of lumps the size of peas and walnut halves. If it seems too dry, gradually add water, 1/2 tablespoon at a time. If it seems too wet, add more semolina flour, 1 tablespoon at a time.

When the dough is the proper consistency, extrude according to the manufacturer's instructions.

When the Maquechou is almost ready, cook pasta in boiling water 2 to 6 minutes. Drain pasta.

Maquechou

YIELD: *4 servings*

2 tablespoons corn oil
1 1/2 cups minced onions
1 clove garlic, minced
1 small green bell pepper, minced
1 small red bell pepper, minced
3 cups frozen or fresh corn kernels
    (about 4 ears of corn)

1 large ripe tomato, peeled, seeded,
    and coarsely chopped (see
    Note, page 77)
1/4 cup water
1/8 teaspoon salt
1/4 teaspoon Tabasco sauce or to
    taste

Heat oil in a large stockpot over medium-high heat. Add onions and garlic and sauté until onions are translucent, about 8 to 10 minutes. Add the green and red bell peppers and cook 2 minutes.

Add corn and tomato and cook 2 to 3 minutes, until the tomato begins to release its juice. Add water, salt, and Tabasco sauce and stir to combine, then bring the mixture to a boil over high heat. Cover, reduce heat, and simmer about 15 minutes.

To serve, place pasta on individual plates and spoon a generous amount of maquechou over each portion.

Chestnut Pasta with Chestnut-Mushroom Delight

I recently discovered the wonders of chestnut flour and dried chestnuts, available in Italian groceries and natural food stores or by mail order (see "Sources," pages 197–198). Although I enjoy eating chestnuts, roasting and peeling them is a less than fun way to prepare ingredients for a meal. Dried chestnuts are a wonderful alternative. Soak the dried chestnuts overnight, then cook them 10 minutes in a pressure cooker or 30 minutes in boiling water, and you get marvelous-tasting chestnuts with minimal work. Use 3 cups of water for 1/2 pound of dried chestnuts.

Another, more expensive but speedier, alternative is a jar of roasted, peeled chestnuts. These are also available in Italian markets and natural food stores. They taste wonderful and add an instant touch of class to a dish.

Chestnut flour has a slightly sweet, appealing flavor. Note that chestnut pasta cooks quickly, even after being refrigerated.

I like to use the fettuccine die for this pasta.

Other recommended accompaniments: Beurre Rouge (page 163), Green Bean–Red Onion Sauce (page 55), Rosemary-Garlic Sauce (page 167), Walnut–Goat Cheese Sauce (page 35).

Makes 6 servings.

Chestnut Pasta

YIELD: *16 ounces*

3/4 cup chestnut flour
3/4 cup semolina flour
1 cup all-purpose flour

1 large egg
1/3 to 1/2 cup red wine

Combine flours in pasta machine bowl. Mix 1 minute, until blended.

Beat egg in a measuring cup. Add enough wine to make 2/3 cup and mix to blend with a fork.

With pasta machine running, slowly add 1/2 cup of the egg mixture over a period of 3 minutes. Let machine continue to mix another minute. The dough should consist of lumps the size of peas and walnut halves. If it seems too dry, gradually add remaining egg mixture, then more wine, 1/2 tablespoon at a time. If it seems too wet, add more semolina flour, 1 tablespoon at a time.

When the dough is the proper consistency, extrude according to the manufacturer's instructions.

When sauce is almost ready, cook pasta in boiling water 1 to 3 minutes. Drain pasta.

Chestnut-Mushroom Delight

YIELD: *6 servings*

1 tablespoon unsalted butter
1 tablespoon olive oil
1/2 cup diced shallots
1 pound mushrooms, stems trimmed,
    cut into 1/8-inch slices
24 canned or cooked dried or fresh
    chestnuts, cut in half

1/2 cup red wine
1/2 cup water
1/4 teaspoon salt
1/4 teaspoon freshly ground black
    pepper
1/4 teaspoon fresh thyme (about 4
    sprigs) or 1/8 teaspoon dried

Heat butter and olive oil in a large skillet over medium heat. Add shallots and cook until translucent, about 5 minutes.

Add sliced mushrooms, stirring to coat with shallots. Cook over medium heat 7 to 10 minutes, until mushrooms begin to release their juice. Add mushrooms, wine, water, salt, pepper, and thyme and stir to combine. Bring to a boil and boil 1 minute, then reduce heat and simmer, uncovered, 10 minutes. Taste and adjust seasonings. Toss with drained pasta and serve immediately.

Chickpea Pasta with Indian Karhi Sauce and Chickpeas

Chickpea noodles are an Indian delicacy. Chickpea flour, called besan, *can be found in natural food stores and Indian markets or can be ordered by mail (see "Sources," pages 197–198). Karhi sauce (also called* kadhi*) is traditionally made with yogurt and chickpea flour; the flour keeps the yogurt from curdling as it heats. This recipe was adapted from Yamuna Devi's* Lord Krishna's Cuisine: The Art of Indian Vegetarian Cooking *(Dutton, 1987).*

Use the spaghetti die and cut the pasta at 1/2-inch to 1-inch lengths. The original recipe calls for ajwain seeds, a difficult-to-find Indian spice with a flavor vaguely reminiscent of oregano. I made the noodles with oregano, and was pleased with the results. The recipe makes a generous amount of sauce, and the resulting dish is like a stew or thick soup.

Other recommended accompaniments: Cilantro-Lime Pesto (page 59), Curried Lentil Soup (page 29), Watercress, Fresh Mozzarella, and Lime Vinaigrette (page 45), Mango Chutney Sauce (page 161).

Makes 4 servings.

Chickpea Pasta

YIELD: *6 ounces*

1 1/4 cups chickpea flour
1/4 teaspoon salt
1/4 teaspoon dried oregano, crumbled
1/4 teaspoon ground cumin

1/2 teaspoon paprika
1 1/2 teaspoons unsalted butter, melted
About 4 tablespoons water

Combine chickpea flour, salt, oregano, cumin, and paprika in pasta machine bowl. Mix 1 minute, until blended.

With pasta machine running, slowly add melted butter. With pasta machine running, add 4 tablespoons water over a period of 3 minutes. Let machine continue to mix another minute. The dough should consist of lumps the size of peas and walnut halves.

If it seems too dry, gradually add more water, 1/2 tablespoon at a time. If it seems too wet, add more chickpea flour, 1 tablespoon at a time.

When the dough is the proper consistency, extrude according to the manufacturer's instructions.

When the sauce is almost ready, cook pasta in boiling water 6 to 8 minutes. Drain pasta.

Indian Karhi Sauce and Chickpeas

YIELD: *4 servings*

3 tablespoons chickpea flour
1/2 teaspoon ground cumin
3/4 teaspoon ground coriander
3/4 teaspoon turmeric
1/4 teaspoon cayenne pepper
3/4 teaspoon salt
1 1/2 cups water

1 1/2 cups plain yogurt
1 tablespoon unsalted butter
1/2 teaspoon mustard seeds
1 (15-ounce) can chickpeas,
    drained and rinsed
2 tablespoons chopped fresh
    cilantro

Mix together the chickpea flour, cumin, coriander, turmeric, cayenne, and salt. Add 3 tablespoons of the water to chickpea flour mixture and whisk to form a smooth paste.

Whisk together remaining water and yogurt. Slowly pour it into the chickpea flour mixture, whisking constantly until smooth.

Pour mixture into a 4-quart saucepan. Heat over medium-high heat, stirring frequently. Bring to a boil, then reduce heat and simmer 10 minutes. Add drained chickpea pasta and simmer 4 minutes.

Meanwhile, melt butter in a medium skillet over medium-high heat. Add the mustard seeds and stir 30 seconds, then add the chickpeas. Sauté 2 minutes or until chickpeas are heated through. Add chickpea mixture to the pasta and sauce. Serve immediately in deep bowls, garnished with chopped cilantro.

Caraway-Rye Pasta with Mustard Vinaigrette and Corned Beef

When thinking of new pasta flavors to create, I am inspired by favorite foods. And for a good sandwich, it's hard to beat corned beef on rye. The only extra I like is mustard, and maybe lettuce and tomato, if I am feeling fanciful.

The pronounced rye flavor of the pasta is delicious with the mustardy vinaigrette and salty bits of corned beef. For added garnishes, add chopped tomatoes or a cup of drained sauerkraut. Serve with a side of pickle spears, of course.

Note that this pasta cooks relatively quickly. I like to make it using the lasagne die, cutting the pasta into 3/4-inch lengths.

Other recommended accompaniments: Edam Cheese Sauce (page 21), Gorgonzola Sauce (page 155), Beef 'n' Beer Goulash (page 115).

Makes 4 servings.

Caraway-Rye Pasta

YIELD: *16 ounces*

1 1/4 cups semolina flour
1 1/4 cups rye flour
2 1/2 teaspoons caraway seeds

3 eggs, lightly beaten together
Water, as needed

Combine flours and caraway seeds in pasta machine bowl. Mix 1 minute, until blended.

With pasta machine running, slowly add most of the eggs, reserving a few tablespoons, over a period of 3 minutes. Let machine continue to mix another minute. The dough should consist of lumps the size of peas and walnut halves. If it seems too dry, gradually add remaining eggs, then water, 1/2 tablespoon at a time. If it seems too wet, add more semolina flour, 1 tablespoon at a time.

When the dough is the proper consistency, extrude according to the manufacturer's instructions.

When the vinaigrette is ready, cook pasta in boiling water 1 to 2 minutes. Drain pasta and place in a large bowl.

Mustard Vinaigrette and Corned Beef

YIELD: *4 servings*

1/2 teaspoon salt
1/4 teaspoon freshly ground black
   pepper
1 tablespoon grainy mustard or
   1 tablespoon Dijon mustard
   plus 1/2 teaspoon mustard seeds

3 tablespoons freshly squeezed
   lemon juice
3 tablespoons extra-virgin olive oil
4 ounces thinly sliced lean corned
   beef, cut into 1 x 1/4-inch
   strips

Combine all ingredients except corned beef in a jar with a tight-fitting lid and shake until well combined. Alternatively, combine in a bowl and whisk thoroughly.

Pour vinaigrette over drained pasta and toss with corned beef strips, making sure to coat everything with vinaigrette. Serve warm, room temperature, or chilled.

Rice Pasta with Pad Thai

Commercially available rice noodles are made from rice flour and water, using a procedure that cannot be duplicated with an automatic pasta machine. Believe me, I tried, but every rice-flour-water pasta I made, while fine-looking in its uncooked state, rapidly turned into a glutinous mush once cooked, no matter how short the cooking time. But when rice flour combines with wheat flour, it becomes more manageable, and I was ultimately pleased with the results. Note, however, that this pasta is very easily overcooked, once cooked, is best served immediately. As the noodles sit in the sauce, they gradually become softer. While they do not loose their shape entirely (as with the failed 100-percent rice noodles), their texture becomes less pleasing after a few hours.

Pad Thai is a traditional Thai dish, a room-temperature salad of rice noodles. Nam pla, or Thai fish sauce, is an essential ingredient. If you can't find it, substitute 2 table-spoons of soy sauce and 1 tablespoon of Worcestershire sauce in the sauce recipe.

I recommend making this pasta with the linguine or fettuccine die.

Other recommended accompaniments: Chicken Soup (page 107), Honey-Lemon Chicken (page 111), Lemon-Ginger Sauce (page 128), Stir-Fried Vegetables (page 63).

Makes 6 servings.

Rice Pasta

YIELD: *16 ounces*

1 1/2 cups all-purpose flour   1/2 to 3/4 cup water
1 cup rice flour

Combine flours in pasta machine bowl. Mix 1 minute, until blended.

With pasta machine running, slowly add 1/2 cup of the water over a period of 3 minutes. Let machine continue to mix another minute. The dough should consist of lumps the size of peas and walnut halves. If it seems too dry, gradually add more water, 1/2 tablespoon at a time. If it seems too wet, add more all-purpose flour, 1 tablespoon at a time.

When the dough is the proper consistency, extrude according to the manufacturer's instructions.

When the Pad Thai is ready, cook pasta in boiling water 1 minute. Drain and immediately rinse pasta under cold water until all the noodles are cool. Use immediately for Pad Thai or other sauces.

Pad Thai

YIELD: *6 servings*

3 tablespoons *nam pla* (Thai fish sauce)
3 tablespoons fresh lime juice
1 tablespoon dark brown sugar
1 tablespoon peanut butter
About 1 tablespoon peanut oil
3 cloves garlic, minced
1/2 teaspoon red pepper flakes or to taste
8 ounces boneless, skinless chicken breast, cut into 1/2-inch cubes

8 ounces extra-firm tofu, cut into 1/2-inch cubes
2 eggs

GARNISHES
1/2 cup chopped roasted peanuts
2 green onions, white and green parts, coarsely chopped
1 cup mung bean sprouts
1 lime, cut into 6 wedges

Stir together nam pla, lime juice, and brown sugar until sugar dissolves.

Add peanut butter to another bowl and gradually stir nam pla mixture into the peanut butter, 1 tablespoon at a time, to ensure a smooth sauce. Add to cooled pasta as soon as it is ready. Do not wash the bowl.

Heat 1 tablespoon peanut oil in a large nonstick skillet over medium heat. Add garlic and red pepper flakes and cook, stirring, 30 seconds. Add chicken and tofu and sauté until the chicken is cooked through, about 5 minutes. Add this to the noodle mixture and stir.

Lightly beat eggs in the bowl you used to mix the sauce. Heat skillet over medium-high heat and add 1 teaspoon oil, if needed. Pour eggs into skillet to form a large pancake shape. Cook until set, then carefully use a spatula to flip it over. Cook on second side 30 to 45 seconds, then remove to a plate. Let cool slightly, then cut into julienne strips and mix with noodle mixture.

To serve, divide pasta onto 6 plates. Garnish with peanuts, green onions, bean sprouts, and lime wedges. Serve immediately.

Oatmeal Pasta with Maple-Walnut Sauce

This is a comfort-food dish, a morning pasta combining oats and maple syrup. Kids will enjoy the sweetness and the pasta cut into spaghetti. I like using papardelle, cut into 1-inch squares. For an extra indulgence, drizzle a tablespoon of cream over each serving.

Other recommended accompaniments: Mango Chutney Sauce (page 161), Pear Vinaigrette and Greens (page 137), Pumpkin-Cider Sauce (page 135), Sherried Apples and Pecans (page 169).

Makes 4 servings.

Oatmeal Pasta

YIELD: *16 ounces*

3 1/2 cups rolled oats or 2 1/2 cups oat flour

2 eggs

About 2 tablespoons milk

If using oatmeal, place in the bowl of a food processor. Process on high 5 minutes, until oats are ground to a fine flour. There should be slightly more than 2 1/2 cups oat flour.

Lightly beat eggs with 2 tablespoons milk.

Place 2 1/2 cups oat flour in pasta machine bowl. Mix 1 minute, until blended.

With pasta machine running, slowly add egg mixture over a period of 3 minutes. Let machine continue to mix another minute. The dough should consist of lumps the size of peas and walnut halves. If it seems too dry, gradually add milk, 1/2 tablespoon at a time. If it seems too wet, add more oat flour, 1 tablespoon at a time.

When the dough is the proper consistency, extrude according to the manufacturer's instructions.

When the sauce is ready, cook pasta in boiling water 1 to 4 minutes. Drain pasta.

Maple-Walnut Sauce

YIELD: *4 servings*

1/2 cup pure maple syrup	1 teaspoon pure vanilla extract
2 tablespoons unsalted butter	1/4 cup chopped walnuts
Pinch of salt	1/4 cup heavy cream (optional)

Place maple syrup and butter in a small saucepan and heat over medium-low heat until butter melts. Increase heat to medium and boil 1 minute, then reduce heat and add salt and vanilla. Boil 1 minute, then reduce heat and add walnuts. Simmer 3 minutes, then remove from heat. The sauce should be warm when you pour it on the pasta. To serve, divide pasta into 4 bowls. Ladle on sauce. If desired, drizzle each serving with 1 tablespoon heavy cream.

Millet Pasta with Lemony Chard, Leeks, and Currants

Millet is an ancient grain, mentioned in the Bible. It is highly nutritious, containing magnesium and iron as well as B vitamins. The flavor is mild, slightly nutty, and it gives the pasta a pale yellow color. Millet flour is available in natural food stores or by mail (see "Sources," pages 197–198). This pasta works well with the fettuccine, linguine, or spaghetti dies.

Other recommended accompaniments: Fresh Fennel–Anchovy Sauté (page 65), Green Bean–Red Onion Sauce (page 55), Lamb and Chickpea Stew (page 117), Zucchini Mélange (page 57).

Makes 6 servings.

Millet Pasta

YIELD: *about 16 ounces*

1 1/4 cups all-purpose flour
1 1/4 cups millet flour

2 large eggs
2 to 6 tablespoons water

Combine flours in pasta machine bowl. Mix 1 minute, until blended.

Break eggs into a measuring cup and lightly beat with 2 tablespoons water.

With pasta machine running, slowly add egg mixture over a period of 3 minutes. Let machine continue to mix another minute. The dough should consist of lumps the size of peas and walnut halves. If it seems too dry, gradually add water, 1/2 tablespoon at a time. If it seems too wet, add more all-purpose flour, 1 tablespoon at a time.

When the dough is the proper consistency, extrude according to the manufacturer's instructions.

When the chard mixture is almost ready, cook pasta in boiling water 5 to 7 minutes. Drain pasta.

Lemony Chard, Leeks, and Currants

YIELD: *6 servings*

1 tablespoon unsalted butter
1 tablespoon extra-virgin olive oil
3 leeks, white and pale green parts
    only, quartered and thinly
    sliced, well rinsed
12 ounces red chard

1/4 cup currants
1/4 teaspoon salt
1/4 teaspoon freshly ground black
    pepper
2 tablespoons fresh lemon juice
1 tablespoon water

Heat butter and olive oil in a large skillet over medium heat. Add leeks and cook 10 to 12 minutes or until soft and translucent.

Meanwhile, prepare chard: Rinse each leaf under cool running water, ensuring that no grit clings to the leaves. Do not dry leaves. Tear the tip of each leaf, then tear leaves from stems. Chop leaves and set aside. Trim the bottom of each stem, then thinly slice the stems.

Add chard stems, currants, salt, pepper, lemon juice, and water to the leeks. Stir, cover, and cook 3 to 5 minutes or until stems are softened. Stir, then add chard leaves. Cover, cook 1 minute, then stir to mix the leaves and stem mixture. Re-cover and cook over medium heat 3 to 4 minutes or until leaves are tender. Toss immediately with drained pasta and serve.

From Land to Sea

Pasta is an ideal food for those who desire to reduce the amount of meat they consume. It is easy to eat less meat, chicken, and seafood when they are served with pasta, a natural accompaniment for these foods.

The recipes in this chapter use various broths, spices, herbs, and juices for flavoring, and are served with easy-to-prepare meat-, chicken-, and seafood-based dishes.

Olive Pasta Niçoise

I love the refreshing flavors of salade niçoise—*potatoes, pungent olives, salty anchovies, tuna, and green beans. The olives in the pasta make this a unique pasta salad with a French twist. This recipe makes a lot, and is great warm or cold. Leftovers will be appreciated.*

This pasta salad requires a few more steps than some other recipes, but the results are worth it. It is easiest to make if you have a metal pasta strainer that fits into the pot for boiling water. Start the water boiling while you prepare the pasta. Boil the potatoes and then the green beans, as instructed below, to help save time. You can use the same water for the green beans, potatoes, and pasta

I found this salad works best when the pasta is cut into macaroni, penne, or ziti shapes—bite-size pieces to go with the chunks of vegetables.

Other recommended accompaniments: Fresh Fennel–Anchovy Sauté (page 65), Puttanesca Sauce (page 139), Roasted Red Pepper Sauce (page 25).

Makes 8 servings.

Olive Pasta

YIELD: *16 ounces*

20 kalamata olives (see Note, opposite), pitted
1 1/4 cups semolina flour

1 1/4 cups all-purpose flour
6 to 8 tablespoons water

Process olives in a blender or mini food processor until pureed.

Combine flours in pasta machine bowl. Mix 1 minute, until blended. Add pureed olives and mix 1 minute, until evenly distributed.

With pasta machine running, slowly add 6 tablespoons water over a period of 3 minutes. Let machine continue to mix another minute. The dough should consist of lumps the size of peas and walnut halves. If it seems too dry, gradually add more water, 1/2 tablespoon at a time. If it seems too wet, add more semolina flour, 1 tablespoon at a time.

When the dough is the proper consistency, extrude according to the manufacturer's instructions.

When Niçoise salad and dressing are ready, cook pasta in boiling water 2 to 6 minutes. Drain pasta and rinse with cold water.

Niçoise Mix

YIELD: *8 servings*

VINAIGRETTE DRESSING
7 tablespoons fresh lemon juice
7 tablespoons extra-virgin olive oil
1/2 teaspoon salt
1/2 teaspoon freshly ground pepper
1 teaspoon dry mustard

SALAD
1 pound green beans, ends trimmed,
    cut into 1 1/2-inch lengths
6 small new potatoes
1 (6-ounce) can water-packed tuna
8 anchovies, cut into 1/4-inch pieces
6 kalamata olives, pitted and sliced
16 cherry tomatoes, halved, for
    garnish
2 hard-cooked eggs, quartered, for
    garnish

Prepare dressing: Combine all ingredients in a blender or a jar with a tight-fitting lid. If using a blender, blend until smooth. If using a jar, shake until ingredients are smoothly mixed. Dressing will keep in refrigerator several days. Makes 1 cup.

Prepare salad: Cook green beans in boiling water about 5 minutes or until crisp-tender. Remove beans with a slotted spoon and rinse under cold running water to stop cooking. Place beans in a large bowl and toss with 2 tablespoons of the dressing.

Cook potatoes in boiling water 10 to 15 minutes or until they can be pierced easily with a knife. Remove with a slotted spoon and rinse under cold running water to stop cooking. Cut into bite-size pieces. Add to the green beans and toss with an additional 2 tablespoons dressing. Add tuna, anchovies, and olives, and toss with an additional 1 tablespoon dressing.

Add drained pasta to the vegetable mix. Toss with an additional 3 tablespoons dressing. Serve immediately or chill for several hours to cool. If serving chilled, add more dressing before serving if the salad seems dry.

To serve, place 1 cup of the salad on each plate and garnish with 4 cherry tomato halves and a hard-cooked egg quarter.

Note It is important to use good-quality, flavorful olives for this pasta. The pitted canned California variety just doesn't offer the right flavor.

Very Dill Pasta with Poached Salmon and Spinach Beurre Blanc

When I think of dill, I always think of salmon, with which it is often paired. This is a well-balanced one-dish meal—starch (pasta), vegetable (spinach), and protein (salmon)— bound together in a most delicious way with beurre blanc, *a French butter and wine sauce. This dish is best served as soon as it is made.*

Other recommended accompaniments: Asparagus, Leeks, and Red Peppers (page 33), Cucumber Sauce (page 51), Rosy Vegetable Sauce (page 27), Mushroom-Herb Pesto (page 39).

Makes 4 servings.

Very Dill Pasta

YIELD: *16 ounces*

1 1/4 cups semolina flour
1 1/4 cups all-purpose flour
1/2 cup chopped fresh dill

3 large eggs, lightly beaten
Water, as needed

Combine flours in pasta machine bowl. Mix 1 minute, until blended. Add dill and mix 1 minute, until evenly distributed.

With pasta machine running, slowly add eggs, reserving 2 tablespoons, over a period of 3 minutes. Mixture will be lumpy, and, depending on your machine, you may need a spatula to help it go through. Let machine continue to mix another minute. The dough should consist of lumps the size of peas and walnut halves. If it seems too dry, gradually add more egg, then water, 1/2 tablespoon at a time. If it seems too wet, add more semolina flour, 1 tablespoon at a time.

When the dough is the proper consistency, extrude according to the manufacturer's instructions.

When sauce is almost ready, cook pasta in boiling water 2 to 6 minutes. Drain pasta and place in a large bowl.

Poached Salmon and Spinach Beurre Blanc

YIELD: *4 servings*

1 cup dry white wine
1 cup water
1 leek, white part only, minced
1 large carrot, minced
1 stalk celery, minced
4 (6-ounce) salmon fillets
1/4 teaspoon salt
6 tablespoons unsalted butter, cut
    into 12 pieces

1 (10-ounce) package frozen
    chopped spinach, cooked
    according to package
    instructions, excess liquid
    squeezed out
1 tablespoon finely chopped fresh dill
    or 2 teaspoons dried dill weed

Combine wine, water, leek, carrot, and celery in a large saucepan over medium-high heat. Bring to a boil, reduce heat, and simmer, covered, 20 minutes. Remove lid and carefully add salmon fillets to simmering liquid. Cover and cook over medium-low heat 8 to 10 minutes or until salmon is opaque and flakes easily with a fork. Remove salmon to an oven-safe plate, cover with foil, and keep it warm in a low 200F (95C) oven while preparing sauce.

Strain vegetables from liquid and reserve. Pour the liquid into a small saucepan, add salt, and bring to a boil. Boil until liquid is reduced to 2 tablespoons, about 5 minutes. Drop 2 pieces of butter into the reduced liquid and cook over low heat, stirring, until butter is melted and incorporated. Repeat with remaining butter, adding 2 pieces at a time, until all the butter is added. Stir in chopped spinach and dill.

To serve, divide the pasta among 4 plates. Top each plate of pasta with a salmon fillet and garnish with reserved vegetables. Ladle sauce over salmon and pasta. Serve immediately.

Old Bay Pasta with Sweet-and-Sour Sardines

Old Bay Seasoning is a classic seafood seasoning made with a combination of secret spices that includes celery salt, mustard, pepper, laurel (bay) leaves, cloves, pimiento, ginger, mace, cardamom, cassia, and paprika. It can usually be found by the seafood department of most markets.

Sardines are a meaty, assertive fish that go well with the bold flavors of this pepper-and-onion sauté. You can serve this dish hot or at room temperature. This recipe works well with the spaghetti, linguine, or fettuccine dies.

Other recommended accompaniments: Edam Cheese Sauce (page 21), Lemony Chard, Leeks, and Currants (page 95), Maquechou (page 83).

Makes 4 servings.

Old Bay Pasta

YIELD: *16 ounces*

1 1/4 cups semolina flour
1 1/4 cups all-purpose flour
1 tablespoon Old Bay Seasoning

3 large eggs, lightly beaten together
2 to 4 tablespoons orange juice

Combine flours in pasta machine bowl. Mix 1 minute, until blended. Add Old Bay Seasoning and mix 1 minute, until evenly distributed.

Mix together eggs and 2 tablespoons orange juice.

With pasta machine running, slowly add egg mixture, reserving 2 tablespoons, over a period of 3 minutes. Let machine continue to mix another minute. The dough should consist of lumps the size of peas and walnut halves. If it seems too dry, gradually add remaining egg mixture, then orange juice, 1/2 tablespoon at a time. If it seems too wet, add more semolina flour, 1 tablespoon at a time.

When the dough is the proper consistency, extrude according to the manufacturer's instructions.

When sardines are almost ready, cook pasta in boiling water 2 to 6 minutes. Drain pasta.

Sweet-and-Sour Sardines

YIELD: *4 servings*

2 tablespoons extra-virgin olive oil
1 large onion, cut in half crosswise
    and thinly sliced lengthwise
1 red bell pepper, thinly sliced
1 green bell pepper, thinly sliced
1 large orange with skin, rinsed,
    cut in half lengthwise and thinly
    sliced crosswise
1 large tomato, chopped, or 3
    canned plum tomatoes,
    drained and chopped

1/4 cup raisins
1/8 teaspoon ground cloves
2 bay leaves
salt
1 (3 3/4-ounce) can sardines,
    preferably water-packed,
    drained

Heat olive oil in a large saucepan over medium-high heat. Add onion and cook, stirring occasionally, until translucent and edges begin to brown, about 20 minutes.

Add bell peppers and cook until softened, about 8 minutes. Reserve 4 slices of orange and set aside for garnish. Add remaining orange and tomato, with all their juices. Stir and add raisins, cloves, bay leaves, and salt. Bring to a boil, then simmer over low heat, uncovered, until all the vegetables are soft, about 10 to 15 minutes. (Sauce may be prepared in advance up to this point. Refrigerate, covered, overnight. Reheat before adding sardines.)

Stir in sardines and cook just until sardines are heated through.

To serve, divide pasta onto 4 plates and top with sardine mixture. Garnish with reserved orange slices.

Saffron Pasta with Sole Amandine

This dish is a snap to make, and the buttery almonds go beautifully with the golden pasta and sole for a great quick yet elegant dinner. Sole is not widely available in the United States; flounder may be substituted. I like lots of almonds, so I call for a generous amount here, but fewer may be used.

I prefer to use lightly salted butter here, because it seems to have just the right amount of salt for this dish. Unsalted butter with added salt doesn't yield the same flavors.

The saffron threads need to soak about 20 minutes to impart their full flavor. Use the fettuccine or linguine dies for this recipe.

Other recommended accompaniments: Coconut-Squash Sauce (page 31), Creamed Leeks (page 159), Indian Braised Potatoes (page 71), Vegetable Soup (page 173).

Makes 4 servings.

Saffron Pasta

YIELD: *16 ounces*

1 1/4 cups semolina flour
1 1/4 cups all-purpose flour
1/4 teaspoon saffron threads, soaked in
    1 tablespoon boiling water
    20 minutes

3 large eggs, lightly beaten together
Water, as needed

Combine flours in pasta machine bowl. Mix 1 minute, until blended. Turn off machine and drizzle saffron water over flour mixture.

With pasta machine running, slowly add eggs, reserving 2 tablespoons, over a period of 3 minutes. Let machine continue to mix another minute. The dough should consist of lumps the size of peas and walnut halves. If it seems too dry, gradually add remaining egg, then water, 1/2 tablespoon at a time. If it seems too wet, add more semolina flour, 1 tablespoon at a time.

When the dough is the proper consistency, extrude according to the manufacturer's instructions.

When sole is almost ready, cook pasta in boiling water 2 to 6 minutes. Drain pasta.

Sole Amandine

YIELD: *4 servings*

4 (6-ounce) sole fillets, skin removed
Salt and freshly ground black pepper
1/4 cup lightly salted butter
1 cup slivered almonds
2 tablespoons minced fresh parsley,
    for garnish

Lemon wedges or other citrus, such
    as lime or orange wedges, for
    garnish

Sprinkle both sides of sole with salt and pepper. Melt butter in a large skillet over medium heat. Add sole and sauté until lightly browned on each side. Remove sole to an oven-safe plate, cover with foil, and keep warm in a low (200F, 95C) oven.

Heat butter remaining in pan over medium heat and add almonds. Sauté until light gold, 2 to 3 minutes; remove from heat. Remove 1/4 cup of almonds and set aside. Add drained pasta to pan and toss with almonds.

To serve, divide pasta among 4 plates. Spoon sole fillets on top of pasta. Spoon 1 tablespoon of reserved almonds over each fillet. Sprinkle with parsley and serve with a lemon wedge on the side.

Chicken Noodles with Chicken Soup

Chicken soup is the penultimate comfort food, topped only by chicken noodle soup. This brings back memories of childhood, when a bowl of chicken noodle soup was, to my mind, the ideal food for lunch or dinner. I recommend using the linguine die for these noodles.

Pressure cookers shine when it comes to stock. Chicken stock normally takes 3 hours; in a pressure cooker it takes under an hour. I do offer instructions for both methods. I recommend not including salt in your stock, unless you are going to eat it plain, as a broth. This way you can adjust the salt as necessary in your soup recipe.

The best chicken pieces to use for stock are those with lots of bones. I use necks and breast bones with a little meat still attached, from which most of the meat was removed by the butcher for the packages of boneless breasts—some butchers offer this option. Bones are what gives the stock flavor. Use as little skin as possible, to reduce the amount of fat.

Other recommended accompaniments: Chicken Mole Sauce (page 69), Honey-Lemon Chicken (page 111), Lemon-Ginger Sauce (page 128), Pad Thai (page 91).

Makes 8 servings.

Chicken Noodles

YIELD: *16 ounces*

1 1/4 cups semolina flour
1 1/4 cups all-purpose flour
1 large egg

1/2 cup chicken stock (from below),
at room temperature

Combine flours in pasta machine bowl. Mix 1 minute, until blended.

Whisk together egg and chicken stock in a measuring cup.

With pasta machine running, slowly add 1/2 cup egg mixture over a period of 3 minutes. Let machine continue to mix another minute. The dough should consist of lumps the size of peas and walnut halves. If it seems too dry, gradually add remaining egg mixture, 1/2 tablespoon at a time. If it seems too wet, add more semolina flour, 1 tablespoon at a time.

When the dough is the proper consistency, extrude according to the manufacturer's instructions.

When soup is ready, cook pasta in boiling water 2 to 3 minutes if using in the soup until just barely tender to the bite. (The pasta needs the room and amount of liquid to cook initially, but it will continue to cook after adding to the soup.) Drain pasta. (If using with another sauce, cook 2 to 6 minutes and drain.)

Chicken Soup

YIELD: *8 servings*

CHICKEN STOCK

3 pounds chicken (with lots of bones), cut into pieces and extra skin and fat removed

2 carrots, cut into 1-inch chunks

2 celery stalks, cut into 2-inch pieces

1 large onion, coarsely chopped

2 cloves garlic, peeled

4 parsley sprigs

6 peppercorns

1 bay leaf

10 cups water

CHICKEN SOUP

1 pound boneless, skinless chicken meat cut into 1/4-inch dice

1 large carrot, diced

1 celery stalk, diced

1/2 teaspoon salt

1/4 teaspoon freshly ground black pepper

2 quarts chicken stock, minus 1/2 cup to use for pasta

Parsley sprigs, for garnish

Make stock: Place all ingredients in a pressure cooker or stockpot.

For pressure cooker: Cover, securing lid, and bring to high pressure over high heat. Reduce heat to maintain high pressure and cook 30 minutes. Remove from heat and let pressure reduce naturally—this can take 25 to 30 minutes.

When the pressure has dropped, remove lid, being careful to keep it turned away from you to avoid the steam.

For standard stockpot: Place all ingredients in a 6- to 8-quart stockpot. Cover and bring to a boil over high heat. Reduce heat and simmer, covered, about 3 hours.

For either method, let stock cool slightly, then strain, pressing slightly on vegetables to release liquid. Discard the vegetables and the chicken.

If you want to use the stock right away, skim any obvious fat off the surface and discard. Otherwise, refrigerate stock for several hours or overnight and remove any congealed fat from the surface. Chicken stock may be refrigerated up to 3 days or frozen up to 3 months. Makes about 2 quarts.

Make soup: Combine chicken, carrot, celery, salt, pepper, and chicken stock in a stockpot or pressure cooker.

For pressure cooker: Cover, securing lid, and bring to high pressure over high heat. Reduce heat to maintain high pressure and cook 8 minutes. Quick-release the pressure, following manufacturer's directions. Remove the lid, being careful to keep it turned away from you to avoid the steam and check chicken and vegetables. Chicken should be cooked through, with no pink, and the vegetables should be tender. If they are not quite ready, simmer 5 to 10 minutes, as needed, with the lid loose.

For standard stockpot: Bring soup to a boil over high heat. Reduce heat and simmer, covered, 25 to 30 minutes, until chicken is done and vegetables are tender.

Add partially cooked pasta to the soup and cook until tender. To serve, ladle soup into bowls and garnish with fresh parsley sprigs.

Lemon-Pepper Pasta with Honey-Lemon Chicken

When I was growing up in Washington, the only ethnic food available was Chinese. Nowadays, dozens of ethnic groups have opened restaurants, which has caused Chinese restaurants to increase the sophistication of their food. Now we can try many different regional Chinese specialties. But one of my favorite preparations is actually from those bygone days: lemon chicken. These were nuggets of deep-fried chicken, served with a sweetened lemon sauce.

My palate has changed somewhat since my childhood—deep fried *now means "too greasy."* But chicken dipped in egg and flour and lightly fried is very tasty. If possible, use a nonstick skillet to minimize the amount of oil needed. The honey in the sauce adds a pleasing sweetness that goes well with the spiciness of the pepper in the pasta. This recipe works well with the spaghetti, linguine, or fettuccine dies.

Other recommended accompaniments: Vegetable Soup (page 173), Creamy Roasted Tomato Sauce (page 177), Lemon-Ginger Sauce (page 128), Smoked Trout Sauce (page 61).

Makes 4 servings.

Lemon-Pepper Pasta

YIELD: *16 ounces*

1 1/4 cups semolina flour
1 1/4 cups all-purpose flour
1/2 teaspoon freshly grated black pepper
Grated zest of 1 lemon

3 tablespoons fresh lemon juice
About 3 tablespoons water
1 large egg, lightly beaten

Combine flours in pasta machine bowl. Mix 1 minute, until blended. Add pepper and lemon zest and mix 1 minute.

Stir together egg, lemon juice, and 3 tablespoons water and set aside.

With pasta machine running, slowly add egg mixture over a period of 3 minutes, reserving 2 tablespoons. Let machine continue to mix another minute. The dough should consist of lumps the size of peas and walnut halves. If it seems too dry, gradually add remaining egg mixture, then water, 1/2 tablespoon at a time. If it seems too wet, add more semolina flour, 1 tablespoon at a time. Break up larger clumps of dough with a rubber spatula or knife, to ensure even incorporation of the liquid.

When the dough is the proper consistency, extrude according to the manufacturer's instructions.

When chicken is almost ready, cook pasta in boiling water 4 to 6 minutes. Drain pasta.

Honey-Lemon Chicken

YIELD: *4 servings*

2 large boneless, skinless chicken
    breasts (about 1 pound)
1 egg
Grated zest of 1 lemon
1 1/2 teaspoons cornstarch
1 cup chicken or vegetable broth
1/3 cup fresh lemon juice
1/4 cup honey

1/4 teaspoon salt
1/2 teaspoon mustard, preferably
    Chinese hot mustard (available
    in Asian markets)
1 tablespoon peanut oil
1/2 cup all-purpose flour
Lemon wedges, for garnish

Cut the chicken into 1/2-inch cubes. Lightly beat egg and lemon zest together in a bowl. Stir in chicken and set aside.

Add cornstarch to a small saucepan. Stir in a small amount of broth until smooth. Gradually stir in remaining broth, then add lemon juice, honey, salt, and mustard. Cook over medium heat, stirring, until thickened, about 5 to 10 minutes. When sauce coats the back of a spoon, remove from heat and set aside.

Heat peanut oil in a large skillet over medium-high heat. Remove chicken pieces from egg mixture and dredge in flour, shaking off excess, then add to hot oil. Stir-fry until cubes of chicken are golden, about 3 to 5 minutes. Test a piece, cutting into it to ensure that the chicken is opaque and white in center, with no pink remaining. Drain chicken on paper towels. Wipe pan clean, return chicken to pan, and add reserved sauce. Heat over medium-low heat just to warm.

To serve, divide pasta among 4 plates. Top each plate of pasta with a serving of the chicken and honey-lemon sauce. Garnish with lemon wedges.

Cranberry Pasta with American Turkey Fessenjen

Fessenjen is a traditional Persian dish. Meat or poultry, either ground and formed into balls or kept in pieces, is cooked slowly in a sauce that includes pomegranate juice or pomegranate molasses and a generous amount of ground walnuts. While pomegranate juice is available here (Knudsen sells a bottle often carried by natural food stores), it is not always easy to find.

In this recipe, cranberry juice makes a delicious alternative to pomegranate juice as well as a perfect partner for turkey—the all-American pair. The sweetness of the cranberry concentrate helps the pasta to cook quickly, so be careful not to overcook. This recipe was inspired by one created by Copeland Marks, prolific documentor of exotic cuisines, in his book Sephardic Cooking *(Donald I. Fine, 1992). Use the spaghetti and linguine dies.*

Other recommended accompaniments: Orange Butter Sauce (page 43), Pumpkin-Cider Sauce (page 135), Sherried Apples and Pecans (page 169), Sweet-and-Sour Sardines (page 103).

Makes 6 servings.

Cranberry Pasta

YIELD: *16 ounces*

1 1/4 cups semolina flour   1 large egg
1 1/4 cups all-purpose flour
1/3 cup thawed frozen cranberry
    juice concentrate

Combine flours in pasta machine bowl. Mix 1 minute, until blended.

Whisk together cranberry juice concentrate and egg in a measuring cup.

With pasta machine running, slowly add juice mixture, reserving 2 tablespoons, over a period of 3 minutes. Let machine continue to mix another minute. The dough should consist of lumps the size of peas and walnut halves. If it seems too dry, gradually add more juice mixture, 1/2 tablespoon at a time. If it seems too wet, add more semolina flour, 1 tablespoon at a time. Break up larger clumps of dough with a rubber spatula or knife, to ensure even incorporation of the liquid.

When the dough is the proper consistency, extrude according to the manufacturer's instructions.

When turkey is almost ready, cook pasta in boiling water 1 to 4 minutes. Drain pasta.

American Turkey Fessenjen

YIELD: *6 servings*

TURKEY MEATBALLS
1 pound ground turkey
1 medium onion, grated
1/2 teaspoon salt
1/4 teaspoon freshly ground black
    pepper
1 1/2 teaspoons grated ginger root

FESSENJEN SAUCE
1 tablespoon extra-virgin olive oil
2 medium onions, chopped
1 cup walnuts, toasted (see Note,
    page 35) and ground

1/2 teaspoon ground cinnamon
1/4 teaspoon ground cardamom
1/4 teaspoon ground cloves
1/4 teaspoon ground ginger
1/4 teaspoon turmeric
1/2 teaspoon salt
1 (6-ounce) can tomato paste
2 cups cranberry juice
1 cup water
1 teaspoon honey
1 cup dried cranberries or dried
    apricots

Meatballs: Mix together ground turkey, grated onion, salt, pepper, and ginger. Form into about 48 (1-inch) balls.

Spray a large nonstick skillet with cooking spray and heat over medium heat. Add 1/3 of the meatballs and cook briefly on all sides, so they are white and hold their shape, about 3 to 5 minutes. Remove to a plate and repeat with remaining meatballs. Set aside.

Heat olive oil in a large pot over medium-high heat. Add onions and sauté about 3 to 5 minutes, until softened. Stir in walnuts. Add cinnamon, cardamom, cloves, ground ginger, turmeric, and salt and stir to coat the onion mixture with the spices.

Whisk together tomato paste, cranberry juice, water, and honey until smooth. Pour into pot and mix with onion mixture. Stir in cranberries. Add meatballs and stir gently to distribute them evenly, being careful not to break them apart.

Bring meatball mixture to a boil, then reduce heat and simmer, covered, 1 hour, stirring occasionally until sauce is thickened and the meatballs are cooked through. (Meatballs and sauce may be prepared in advance and refrigerated overnight. They also make great leftovers.)

To serve, divide pasta among 6 plates. Place 6 to 8 meatballs on each plate and ladle sauce over them. Serve immediately.

Beer-Paprika Pasta with Beef 'n' Beer Goulash

Hungarian goulash is a slow-simmered stew, most commonly made with beef (though veal and pork are sometimes used). Its distinguishing spice is paprika, which is used generously enough to give the dish both flavor and color. It is often served with noodles, and the beer in this pasta complements the hearty stew, which also has beer in it. I recommend using a dark beer for a richer flavor, but not a stout—it is too strong-flavored. Use the fettuccine or linguine dies.

As with most stews, this one takes a while to cook. You can prepare it the day before you plan to serve it and reheat, which also helps the flavors develop.

Other recommended accompaniments: Chunky Tomato Sauce (page 171), Edam Cheese Sauce (page 21), Mushroom-Herb Pesto (page 39), Sun-Dried Tomato Pesto (page 23).

Makes 4 servings.

Beer-Paprika Pasta

YIELD: *16 ounces*

1 1/4 cups semolina flour
1 1/4 cups all-purpose flour
1 teaspoon paprika, preferably
    Hungarian

1/2 cup flat beer, preferably dark
1 tablespoon extra-virgin olive oil

Combine flours in pasta machine bowl. Mix 1 minute, until blended. Add paprika and mix 1 minute.

Stir together beer and olive oil in a measuring cup.

With pasta machine running, slowly add beer mixture, reserving 2 tablespoons, over a period of 3 minutes. Let machine continue to mix another minute. The dough should consist of lumps the size of peas and walnut halves. If it seems too dry, gradually add more beer mixture, 1/2 tablespoon at a time. If it seems too wet, add more semolina flour, 1 tablespoon at a time. Break up larger clumps of dough with a rubber spatula or knife, to ensure even incorporation of the liquid.

When the dough is the proper consistency, extrude according to the manufacturer's instructions.

When goulash is ready, cook pasta in boiling water 4 to 6 minutes. Drain pasta.

Beef 'n' Beer Goulash

YIELD: *4 servings*

1 tablespoon vegetable oil
1 large onion, quartered and thinly
    sliced crosswise
1 1/2 pounds boneless beef chuck, cut
    into 1-inch cubes
1/2 teaspoon salt
1/2 teaspoon freshly ground black
    pepper
2 cloves garlic, minced
2 tablespoons paprika, preferably
    Hungarian, plus extra for
    garnish

1/2 teaspoon dried marjoram
1/2 teaspoon caraway seeds
1 cup water
1 cup beer
2 tablespoons all-purpose flour
    mixed with 4 tablespoons water
    (optional)

Heat oil in a large saucepan or Dutch oven over medium heat. Add onion and cook, stirring occasionally, until it begins to turn golden and caramelize, about 30 minutes.

Season beef with salt and pepper. Add beef to onion and cook, stirring occasionally, until browned on all sides. Add garlic and cook 3 minutes. Sprinkle paprika, marjoram, and caraway seeds over beef and onion and stir to coat everything with the spices. Add water and beer and mix well. Bring to a boil, then reduce heat and simmer, covered, about 1 1/2 hours or until tender. Remove lid and simmer, allowing some of the liquid to evaporate. (The goulash may be prepared in advance up to this point and refrigerated overnight. The next day, skim off fat that may have congealed and heat over medium heat.)

For a thicker gravy, use a slotted spoon to remove beef and most of the onion from the liquid in the pan. Add flour mixture and cook, stirring, over low heat until thickened, about 5 minutes. Return beef and onion to the pan and cook, stirring, to coat and heat through.

To serve, divide pasta among 4 plates. Spoon goulash into the center of pasta. Sprinkle with additional paprika and serve.

Minted Pasta with Lamb and Chickpea Stew

I like lamb, but I never was a fan of mint jelly. Lamb is a meat that I don't care for with sweet ingredients. However, I do like the flavor of fresh mint, and given the Mediterranean popularity of both lamb (think Greek food) and mint, the two seem to go together naturally.

I cut the lamb into pieces smaller than customary for stew; it fits better with the chickpeas and goes well with the pasta. This pasta works well with the fettuccine or linguine dies.

Other recommended accompaniments: Chunky Tomato Sauce (page 171), Cucumber Sauce (page 51), Indian Karhi Sauce and Chickpeas (page 87), Poached Salmon and Spinach Beurre Blanc (page 101).

Makes 4 servings.

Minted Pasta

YIELD: *16 ounces*

1 1/4 cups semolina flour
1 1/4 cups all-purpose flour
1/4 cup chopped fresh mint leaves

Grated zest of 1 lemon
1 tablespoon extra-virgin olive oil
1/2 cup water

Combine flours in pasta machine bowl. Mix 1 minute, until blended. Add mint leaves and lemon zest and mix 1 minute.

Stir together olive oil and water in a measuring cup.

With pasta machine running, slowly add water mixture, reserving 2 tablespoons, over a period of 3 minutes. Let machine continue to mix another minute. The dough should consist of lumps the size of peas and walnut halves. If it seems too dry, gradually add more water mixture, 1/2 tablespoon at a time. If it seems too wet, add more semolina flour, 1 tablespoon at a time. Break up larger clumps of dough with a rubber spatula or knife, to ensure even incorporation of the liquid.

When the dough is the proper consistency, extrude according to the manufacturer's instructions.

When stew is ready, cook pasta in boiling water 4 to 6 minutes. Drain pasta.

Lamb and Chickpea Stew

YIELD: *4 servings*

1 tablespoon extra-virgin olive oil
1 pound lean lamb shoulder or stew
    meat, cut into 1/2-inch cubes
1 medium onion, diced
1 (15-ounce) can chickpeas, drained
    and rinsed
3/4 cup white wine

2 tablespoons tomato paste
1/4 cup water
1/2 teaspoon salt
1/4 teaspoon freshly ground black
    pepper
1/2 teaspoon dried oregano
1 tablespoon chopped fresh mint

Heat olive oil in a large saucepan over medium-high heat. Add lamb and cook, stirring, until browned on all sides, about 5 to 8 minutes. Add onion and cook until it is translucent, about 5 to 8 minutes. Stir in chickpeas.

Gradually whisk wine into the tomato paste until smooth. When all the wine is mixed in, stir in the water. Pour this liquid over the lamb. Stir in salt, pepper, and oregano. Bring mixture to a boil, then reduce heat, and simmer, covered, 30 minutes, stirring occasionally, or until almost tender. Cook, uncovered, 10 to 15 minutes or until lamb is tender.

To serve, toss pasta with the lamb. Sprinkle each serving with chopped fresh mint.

Tequila Pasta with Garlicky Chili con Carne

The right way to make chili is a hotly contested issue. And a hot contest, too. In fact, there are several chili contests every year. Several books have been written on the topic, with debates regarding ground meat or chopped, the type of meat to use, beans or not, cheese or not. I will not vie with the opinions of people devoted to the food. However, I do have my own preferences: I like ground beef; I like beans; and hold the cheese. The beans here are added at the end, so if you are anti-bean, just don't add them. Chili actually improves with age; if you can make it the day before you plan to eat it, it will taste that much better. It takes about an hour and a half to cook, and the flavors merge and develop during this time.

Although chili is associated with Texas and the Southwest, there are regional specialties throughout the country. In Cincinnati, the specialty is "Five-Way Chili." The chili is served on top of spaghetti, with sides of beans, cheese, onions, and oyster crackers. Chili and pasta seems like a good idea to me; the pasta helps absorb some of the heat, and goes well with this robust not-quite-stew/not-quite-soup dish.

This is a very garlicky chili, inspired by recipes with names like "Chicken with 100 Cloves of Garlic." The garlic is not minced, but kept whole and sautéed with the meat and onions. This gives it a chewy crust, while the inside softens and becomes creamy, as with roasted garlic. Then it absorbs the flavors of the chili sauce and meat, making it as edible and mellow as any vegetable. A dash of tequila in the pasta and the sauce is another secret flavor ingredient. Serve with margaritas, of course.

Spaghetti may be the Cincinnati tradition, but I like this chili with wider noodles, such as fettuccine or papardelle, the better to hold the sauce and bits of meat. It also works well with tubular pastas such as macaroni and ziti.

Other recommended accompaniments: Cilantro-Lime Pesto (page 59), Watercress, Fresh Mozzarella, and Lime Vinaigrette (page 45), Lime-Pistachio Sauce (page 133), Roasted Tomato and Corn Salsa (page 77).

Makes 4 to 6 servings.

Tequila Pasta

YIELD: *16 ounces*

1 1/4 cups semolina flour
1 1/4 cups all-purpose flour
3 tablespoons tequila

1 tablespoon fresh lime juice
1/4 cup water
1 tablespoon extra-virgin olive oil

Combine flours in pasta machine bowl. Mix 1 minute, until blended.

Stir together tequila, lime juice, water, and olive oil in a measuring cup.

With pasta machine running, slowly add tequila mixture, reserving 2 tablespoons, over a period of 3 minutes. Let machine continue to mix another minute. The dough should consist of lumps the size of peas and walnut halves. If it seems too dry, gradually add more tequila mixture, 1/2 tablespoon at a time. If it seems too wet, add more semolina flour, 1 tablespoon at a time. Break up larger clumps of dough with a rubber spatula or knife, to ensure even incorporation of the liquid.

When the dough is the proper consistency, extrude according to the manufacturer's instructions.

When chili is ready, cook pasta in boiling water 4 to 6 minutes. Drain pasta.

Garlicky Chili con Carne

YIELD: *4 to 6 servings*

1 pound ground beef
1 large onion, finely chopped
1 jalapeño chile, seeded and diced
20 cloves garlic, ends trimmed,
    peeled, and left whole
1/4 cup mild chili powder
1 tablespoon cumin
1 teaspoon dried oregano

1/2 teaspoon salt
1/4 teaspoon freshly ground black
    pepper
1 (28-ounce) can tomatoes in
    tomato puree
1/4 cup tequila
1 (15-ounce) can kidney beans
    (optional), rinsed and drained

Crumble ground beef into a large pot over medium heat and cook, stirring to break up beef, until browned and no pink shows. Add onion and cook until translucent, about 10 minutes. Add jalapeño chile and cook about 5 minutes, until it begins to soften. Add garlic and cook until golden brown on the edges.

Sprinkle in chili powder, cumin, oregano, salt, and pepper and stir to coat everything. Add tomatoes, crushing the whole tomatoes with the back of a spoon, and tequila. Stir to mix. Bring to a boil and stir. Reduce heat and simmer, uncovered, 30 minutes, until chili is thick, stirring occasionally.

Stir in beans, if using, and simmer 30 minutes.

Chili may be prepared in advance up to this point. Cool slightly, then refrigerate overnight. Reheat over low heat when ready to eat.

To serve, divide drained pasta among individual deep bowls. Ladle a generous amount of chili over each serving. The chili is a substantial part of the meal here; this is not just pasta with a hint of sauce.

Filled and Layered Pasta

Filled pasta is a special treat. You can make any of the flavored pastas in this book and use them to hold an exciting filling, and create a truly impressive, not to mention substantial and delicious, dish. In this chapter I concentrate on ravioli, because that is the easiest kind of filled pasta to make with your pasta machine.

Ravioli

Ravioli is certainly more labor-intensive than plain pasta and sauce, but it is worth the effort. You can create myriad fillings, as compared to the standard few that are commercially available (cheese, spinach, ground beef). Also, you'll find that homemade cheese ravioli is infinitely better than anything you can buy in the store.

Ravioli Techniques

There are certain techniques necessary to creating better ravioli. First, extrude the pasta using the lasagne die, and cut at about 8-inch lengths. Keep the lasagne sheets covered with a damp towel as you work. Make sure the sheets are entirely covered so that the ends do not dry out. Ravioli may be made using these lasagne sheets as is, but I found that they are very thick. The lasagne sheets are as much as twice the thickness of pastas extruded through other dies, such as fettuccine. When you double up a sheet to hold the filling, you get a higher pasta-to-filling ratio than you might like. Plus, the pasta takes a while to cook, since it is so thick. For these reasons, I recommend rolling the lasagne sheets thinner. Try it both ways, and you will probably like the thinner ravioli better.

Rolling Dough for Ravioli

There are two methods you can use for rolling the lasagne sheets to make ravioli: a rolling pin and a hand-cranked pasta roller. Pasta rollers, which cost about $40 to $60, depending on the brand, are a worthwhile investment and a great accessory to your electric pasta machine.

There are two brands of pasta rollers available: Atlas, which can be found in almost every kitchen-supply store, and Imperia, which is harder to find and more expensive but also sturdier. Both are imported from Italy, and both work well. They consist of two metal rollers set in a metal body which can be clamped to a table. You can adjust the distance between the rollers, depending on how thin you want the dough. There are six settings. The dough is inserted between the rollers and turned with a crank. It's that simple. Both machines offer an optional motor (which costs more than the roller itself) in lieu of the hand crank. Vitantonia is a company that carries both machines and sells them by mail (see "Sources," pages 197–198).

When all the dough has been extruded from the pasta machine, begin rolling the sheets through the pasta rollers, one at a time. Begin rolling on the widest setting, passing the dough through once, and work your way up to setting #2, the second thinnest setting (the thinnest setting produces dough that is too thin to hold the ravioli filling).

Rolling out the lasagne dough with a pasta roller is significantly easier than with a rolling pin, and it ensures that the pasta will have a more even thickness throughout. When you roll by hand using a rolling pin, the amount of pressure you apply to the pasta can vary. It is also more difficult to roll the pasta as thinly as you can with a pasta roller. Nonetheless, the rolling-pin method is a good way to start out. Take a lasagne sheet extruded from the machine and place it on a smooth surface, such as a cutting board or a countertop. Using a rolling pin, press down firmly, rolling the dough lengthwise. Roll it as thin as you feel is possible.

To keep the dough from drying out too much, make the ravioli as you roll out the pasta sheets. Roll out two sheets of comparable lengths, one upon which to place the filling, the other to place on top.

Filling Ravioli

To fill the ravioli, take one sheet of rolled pasta and cover the second with a damp cloth and reserve. Place 1/2 to 3/4 teaspoon of filling about 1/2 inch from the edge of the sheet. Place additional 1/2 or 3/4 teaspoonfuls along the pasta sheet at 1-inch intervals.

Brush the reserved sheet of pasta with 1 egg beaten with 1 tablespoon of water (water only may be used, but the addition of an egg provides a better seal, making it less likely that the ravioli will open while cooking). Place second pasta sheet, egg side down, over pasta sheet with filling. Press dough down around the filling with your fingers, then use a knife to cut midway between each mound of ravioli and trim any uneven edges. Use fork tines to press the edges of the ravioli, forming a more secure seal.

Another piece of equipment that is useful is a ravioli wheel, which is not very expensive. These wheels are available with either fluted or straight edges; the fluted edge is more decorative, and helps seal the ravioli, but I recommend sealing the edges further with the fork tines anyway. Some pasta machines come with a ravioli stamp. You place this over the mound of filling and press down, like a cookie cutter, and it cuts out the ravioli. Ravioli stamps are also available at some kitchenware stores and by mail (see "Sources," pages 197–198). These do form a very good seal, but they tend to leave little excess pasta. If you like wide edges of pasta around your filling, then use the knife or pastry-wheel method.

Storing and Cooking Ravioli

Set finished ravioli on a wire rack until ready to cook. Meat or fish fillings should be refrigerated within 30 minutes of being made. You may use a plate, but moisture often accumulates between the bottom of the ravioli and the plate, so a wire rack is the best bet.

Because ravioli fillings tend to be moist, ravioli should be frozen or cooked within a few hours of preparation. If you need to store them for a few hours, keep them on the wire rack in the refrigerator.

To freeze, place rack of ravioli in the freezer for an hour or so, then place the ravioli in a plastic bag and seal. Ravioli may be kept, frozen, up to 2 months.

Suggested Pasta Doughs for Ravioli

I recommend both the Basic Egg Pasta (page 14) and the Water and Oil Pasta (page 16) for any of the recipes in this chapter. (The Egg White Pasta dough is less flexible, as it contains no fat.) I also offer additional recommendations for each recipe. A 16-ounce recipe of pasta dough can make between 80 and 100 ravioli (if you don't roll the dough thinner, a batch will make about 50 ravioli).

Lasagne

This chapter also includes recipes for lasagne. The noodles should also be rolled thinner for lasagne as instructed above for ravioli. Otherwise a 16-ounce batch of pasta will not produce enough sheets for a pan of lasagne, and the thicker lasagne sheets will not taste as good. Extrude the pasta in 10- or 12-inch lengths for lasagne.

Kugel

There is one recipe for kugel, a traditional Jewish noodle pudding, rich with eggs, butter, and sour cream.

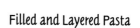

Chicken Velvet Ravioli with Lemon-Ginger Sauce

I used to visit my grandparents in upstate New York for several weeks every summer. Once I turned twelve, my industrious grandmother, Omi, was determined that I learn how to cook, not just the cookies I loved to bake, but dinner as well. One of my favorite dishes to prepare was Chicken Velvet. This was a Chinese-inspired recipe that appeared in an issue of Better Homes & Gardens magazine. A chicken breast was pureed in a blender and mixed with egg whites, then cooked in a skillet on the stovetop. It had a wonderful flavor and a velvety smooth texture—perfect, I thought years later, for ravioli filling. Most chicken fillings for ravioli need to be precooked, but, since the meat here is ground, it cooks just right as the ravioli cooks in boiling water.

The Lemon-Ginger Sauce is inspired in part by one of my favorite soups, the Greek egg-lemon soup that is a chicken-rice soup flavored with lemon and mint and enriched with eggs. I took out the rice and mint, and changed the egg–soup proportions to make it a little more saucelike. Following the Chinese inspiration for Chicken Velvet, I used fresh ginger and green onions for flavor. The results are delectable.

If you have leftover filling, you can form it into patties. Heat 1 tablespoon of oil in a skillet and fry about 5 minutes on each side until chicken is white and opaque all the way through.

Recommended pasta recipes: Spinach Pasta (page 18), Lemon-Parsley Pasta (page 48), Chicken Noodles (page 106), Lemon-Pepper Pasta (page 110).

Other recommended accompaniments: Chicken Soup (page 107), Mushroom-Herb Pesto (page 39), Asparagus, Leeks, and Red Peppers (page 33), Stir-Fried Vegetables (page 63).

Makes 4 to 6 servings.

Chicken Velvet Ravioli

YIELD: *1 1/2 cups filling, enough for about 100 ravioli*

12 ounces boneless, skinless chicken
    breast
3/4 teaspoon cornstarch
1/4 teaspoon salt
4 tablespoons chicken broth
2 teaspoons rice wine or dry sherry

2 egg whites, lightly beaten
16 ounces pasta dough
1 egg, lightly beaten with
    1 tablespoon water, for sealing
    ravioli

Cut away and discard any fat and sinew from the chicken breast. Dice chicken, then place in a blender with cornstarch, salt, chicken broth, and rice wine or sherry.

Blend until smooth. Store refrigerated until ready to use.

Roll and fill the pasta, as directed on pages 122–123. After you have prepared about half the ravioli, refrigerate them, to ensure that the chicken filling stays fresh.

Cook ravioli, in batches, in boiling water in a very large stockpot 10 minutes (15 to 20 minutes, if frozen). Remove 1 ravioli and cut into it. The chicken filling should be firm and white, with the palest hint of pink.

Drain cooked ravioli.

Lemon-Ginger Sauce

Yield: *3 1/3 cups; 4 to 6 servings*

4 green onions, thinly sliced, both
    white and green parts
2 2/3 cups Chicken Stock (page 107)
    or canned low-sodium chicken
    broth

4 teaspoons grated ginger root
4 eggs
1/4 cup fresh lemon juice
Salt, to taste

Reserve some of the green parts of the onions for garnish. Bring stock, green onions, and ginger to a boil in a medium saucepan over high heat. Reduce heat, then simmer to let flavors infuse, about 10 minutes.

Whisk eggs together in a bowl. Whisk in lemon juice, then gradually add 1/2 cup of the simmering stock, whisking constantly, or the hot stock will cook eggs.

Pour egg mixture into remaining stock, stirring constantly. Do not bring to a boil, but simmer over low heat 2 minutes. It should be the consistency of heavy cream. Taste and add salt, if needed.

To serve, divide ravioli among individual dishes. Ladle a generous amount of sauce over each serving and sprinkle reserved green onions on top. Serve immediately.

Variation

Lemon-Ginger Soup Increase amounts as follows: Use 4 green onions, 2 tablespoons ginger, and 6 eggs with 6 cups chicken stock and 6 tablespoons lemon juice. Follow the same instructions for making the sauce. Serve soup with the ravioli in wide bowls.

Mushroom Ravioli with Asparagus-Mushroom Sauce

These ravioli are a mushroom-lover's delight. The filling uses regular cultivated mushrooms, and the sauce has woodsy shiitake mushrooms for a double mushroom treat. The asparagus provides a colorful contrast. The secret ingredient here is Boursin cheese, which adds creaminess and flavor. Regular cream cheese may be substituted; if so, add salt and pepper to taste.

Recommended pasta recipes: Asparagus Pasta (page 32), Mushroom Pasta (page 38), Lemon-Parsley Pasta (page 48), Very Dill Pasta (page 100).

Other recommended accompaniments: Creamed Leeks (page 159), Roasted Red Pepper Sauce (page 25), Smoked Trout Sauce (page 61).

Makes 4 to 6 servings.

Mushroom Ravioli

YIELD: *1 1/4 cups filling, enough for about 80 to 90 ravioli, with some left over*

1 tablespoon unsalted butter
1/2 cup thinly sliced green onions,
    white and about 3 inches of
    pale green part
1 pound mushrooms, minced (may
    be done in a food processor)

3 tablespoons Boursin cheese
16 ounces pasta dough
1 egg, lightly beaten with
    1 tablespoon water, for sealing
    ravioli

Melt butter in a large saucepan over medium-high heat. Add green onions and sauté until translucent, about 5 minutes. Add minced mushrooms and cook, stirring occasionally, until juices are released and then evaporate, 25 to 30 minutes. Watch carefully to make sure mushrooms do not burn.

Remove mushroom mixture from heat and stir in Boursin cheese. Stir until cheese melts and is mixed thoroughly with mushrooms. Set aside. (Filling may be prepared in advance and refrigerated up to 2 days.)

Roll and fill the pasta, as directed on pages 122–123.

When sauce is almost ready, cook ravioli in boiling water in a very large stockpot 7 minutes (10 to 12 minutes, if frozen).

Drain cooked ravioli.

Asparagus-Mushroom Sauce

YIELD: *4 to 6 servings*

1 pound fresh asparagus
1 tablespoon unsalted butter
1/2 cup thinly sliced green onions,
    white and about 3 inches of
    pale green parts
1/2 pound shiitake mushrooms,
    washed, stems removed, and
    thinly sliced

1/4 cup Boursin cheese
1/2 cup milk
1/8 teaspoon salt

Rinse asparagus and break off the woody ends: Bend each end until it breaks off easily and discard ends. Place asparagus, tips all facing the same direction, in an 8-inch-square glass pan. Cover with plastic wrap and microwave on HIGH 3 minutes. Let stand, covered, 1 minute, then remove plastic wrap carefully—the steam is very hot. When asparagus is cool enough to handle, cut into 1-inch lengths and set aside.

Melt butter in a large saucepan over medium-high heat. Add green onions and sauté until translucent, about 5 minutes. Add mushrooms and cook, stirring occasionally, until mushrooms begin to release their juices, about 5 minutes. Cook for 1 or 2 minutes, then add Boursin cheese, stirring to melt. Gradually add milk, about 2 tablespoons at a time, stirring to incorporate. Cook over low heat 2 or 3 minutes to warm. The sauce will be slightly thin. Add asparagus and salt and heat until warm.

To serve, divide ravioli among 4 to 6 individual plates and spoon sauce over each serving.

Spinach-Pistachio Ravioli with Lime-Pistachio Sauce

Pistachios always add a touch of class to a dish. Although they are now widely available, they still feel exotic and special. At one time, pistachios were only available in the shell, salted, but unsalted shelled nuts are now increasingly available. These are easier to use and more suitable for cooking. If you only have salted pistachios, omit the salt from the recipe.

Recommended pasta recipes: Spinach Pasta (page 18), Cilantro Pasta (page 58).

Other recommended accompaniments: Cilantro-Lime Pesto (page 59), Indian Braised Potatoes (page 71), Orange Butter Sauce (page 43), Roasted Peppers and Herbs (page 141).

Yields 4 to 6 servings.

Spinach-Pistachio Ravioli

YIELD: *1 1/4 cups filling, enough for about 80 to 90 ravioli, with some left over*

1 (10-ounce) package frozen spinach, cooked according to package directions, excess liquid squeezed out
1/2 cup shelled pistachios, preferably unsalted
1 cup (4 ounces) shredded Monterey Jack cheese
4 teaspoons fresh lime juice
1/8 teaspoon salt
1/4 teaspoon freshly ground black pepper
Pinch of cayenne pepper
16 ounces pasta dough
1 egg, lightly beaten with 1 tablespoon water, for sealing ravioli

Combine spinach, pistachios, and cheese in the bowl of a food processor. Pulse until blended.

Add lime juice, salt, pepper, and cayenne. Process until smooth. (Filling may be prepared in advance and refrigerated for up to 2 days.)

Roll and fill the pasta, as directed on pages 122–123.

Cook ravioli in boiling water in a very large stockpot 7 minutes (10 to 12 minutes, if frozen).

Drain cooked ravioli.

Lime-Pistachio Sauce

YIELD: *4 to 6 servings*

1/4 cup unsalted butter

3 tablespoons fresh lime juice
(about 2 small limes)

1/8 teaspoon salt

1/2 cup coarsely chopped
pistachios, preferably unsalted

Melt butter in a small saucepan over medium-high heat. Whisk in lime juice and salt and simmer 1 minute over medium heat. Stir in chopped pistachios and sauté 2 minutes, being careful not to burn. To serve, divide cooked ravioli among individual plates. Spoon sauce over ravioli and serve immediately.

Pumpkin Ravioli with Pumpkin-Cider Sauce

This is an elegant, rich dish. Hidden flavors—a touch of sherry, a whisper of sage, a sprinkling of pine nuts—give plain canned pumpkin puree something extra. The sauce has an intense, hearty flavor that speaks of autumn and changing leaves.

Recommended pasta recipes: Tomato Pasta (page 20), Carrot Pasta (page 28), Roasted Butternut Squash Pasta (page 30), Fresh Ginger Pasta (page 62).

Other recommended accompaniments: Browned Butter Sauce (page 157), Coconut-Squash Sauce (page 31), Orange Butter Sauce (page 43), Sherried Apples and Pecans (page 169).

Makes 4 to 6 servings.

Pumpkin Ravioli

YIELD: *1 1/4 cups filling, enough for about 80 to 90 ravioli*

1 tablespoon unsalted butter
1 1/2 teaspoons minced fresh sage or
    1/2 teaspoon dried
1 cup canned pumpkin puree
3 tablespoons cream cheese, softened
1/4 teaspoon salt
Freshly ground black pepper

1 teaspoon dry sherry
2 tablespoons pine nuts, finely
    chopped
16 ounces pasta dough
1 egg, lightly beaten with
    1 tablespoon water, for sealing
    ravioli

Melt butter in a small saucepan over medium heat. Reduce heat and add sage. Sauté 2 minutes and let the sage crisp up a little, if using fresh sage. Remove from heat and set aside.

In a small bowl, beat together pumpkin puree and cream cheese with an electric mixer until smooth. Add butter-sage mixture, salt, a little pepper, and sherry and mix until smooth. Fold in pine nuts. Cover and refrigerate about 30 minutes. (Filling may be prepared in advance and refrigerated up to 2 days.)

Roll and fill the pasta, as directed on pages 122–123.

When sauce is ready, cook ravioli in boiling water in a very large stockpot 7 minutes (10 to 12 minutes, if frozen).

Drain cooked ravioli.

Pumpkin-Cider Sauce

YIELD: *1 1/2 cups; 4 to 6 servings*

4 cups apple cider   1 cup half-and-half
1/2 cup canned pumpkin puree

Pour cider into a medium saucepan and bring to a boil over high heat. Continue boiling until cider is reduced to 1 cup, 15 to 20 minutes. Strain through a fine-mesh strainer to remove all the particles.

Rinse out any particles that may have adhered to saucepan. Return the reduced cider to the clean pan and stir in the pumpkin puree. Cook over low heat until liquid bubbles slightly and reduces to 2/3 cup. It should be the consistency of baby-food puree.

Remove pan from heat and slowly stir in half-and-half. Return to low heat and cook until sauce is heated through and the consistency of heavy cream. (The sauce may be prepared in advance and refrigerated up to 2 days. Reheat over low heat when ready to serve.)

To serve, divide ravioli among 4 to 6 individual plates and ladle sauce over each serving.

Gorgonzola-Walnut Ravioli with Pear Vinaigrette and Greens

Gorgonzola is an assertive cheese, as are most of the blue cheeses. The cream cheese in this filling mellows it slightly, but still allows the full flavor to come through. The toasted walnuts add a bit of crunch for a contrast in textures. Any other kind of blue cheese may be substituted for the Gorgonzola cheese.

In this dish, use a mix of greens—endive, spinach, and butter lettuce. The warm ravioli, with their creamy, nutty filling, work well with the greens mixture. The juicy pears in the dressing are a natural complement to the Gorgonzola cheese.

Recommended pasta recipes: Caramelized-Onion Pasta (page 34), Lemon-Parsley Pasta (page 48), Tangy Chive Pasta (page 50).

Other recommended accompaniments: Creamed Leeks (page 159), Gorgonzola Sauce (page 155), Roasted Garlic Sauce and Peas (page 37), Mushroom-Herb Pesto (page 39).

Makes 4 servings.

Gorgonzola-Walnut Ravioli

YIELD: *2/3 cup filling, enough for about 60 ravioli*

3 ounces Gorgonzola cheese,
    crumbled (about 1/4 cup)
1 (3-ounce) package cream cheese
    (about 1/4 cup, packed)
1/3 cup finely chopped, toasted
    walnuts (see Note, page 35)

12 ounces pasta dough
1 egg, lightly beaten with
    1 tablespoon water, for sealing
    ravioli

Mix Gorgonzola and cream cheese with an electric mixer or wooden spoon until blended. Mixture may be lumpy, but most of the two cheeses should be blended together. Stir in the chopped walnuts. Cover and refrigerate 30 minutes. (Filling may be prepared in advance and refrigerated up to 2 days.)

Roll and fill the pasta, as directed on pages 122–123.

While pears are marinating in the vinaigrette, cook ravioli in boiling water in a very large stockpot 7 minutes (10 to 12 minutes, if frozen).

Drain cooked ravioli.

Pear Vinaigrette and Greens

YIELD: *4 servings*

3 tablespoons fresh lemon juice
1/2 teaspoon salt
1/4 teaspoon freshly ground black pepper
3/4 teaspoon fresh thyme leaves or 1/4 teaspoon dried
4 tablespoons walnut oil

2 pears, peeled, cored, and cut into 1/4-inch chunks
6 cups mixed salad greens (such as mesclun mix or a combination of butter lettuce, endive, and spinach), rinsed, dried, and torn into bite-size pieces

Whisk together lemon juice, salt, pepper, and thyme in a small bowl, then whisk in walnut oil. Drizzle over pears and let stand 15 minutes.

Toss drained ravioli with the pears and vinaigrette. Divide the greens among 4 plates and top with the ravioli and pears. Serve immediately.

Three-Cheese Ravioli with Puttanesca Sauce

Puttanesca sauce was introduced to me by my mother-in-law, Esther Robbins, who makes the best version I have had anywhere, even though it's always a little bit different each time she makes it. She doesn't write down amounts or follow recipes, but this is my approximation of her sauce. Essentially, this is a tomato sauce flavored with capers, anchovies, and good-quality olives.

Ricotta filling is the classic ravioli filling. Often it contains eggs as well as Parmesan cheese, but I prefer the creamier texture of this eggless version. Spinach and various herbs may be added for variety.

Recommended pasta recipes: Tomato Pasta (page 20), Sun-Dried Tomato Pasta (page 22), Caramelized-Onion Pasta (page 34), Olive Pasta (page 98).

Other recommended accompaniments: Roasted Peppers and Herbs (page 141), Vegetable Soup (page 173), Zucchini Mélange (page 57).

Makes 4 to 6 servings.

Three-Cheese Ravioli

YIELD: *1 1/4 cups filling, enough for about 80 to 90 ravioli*

1 cup ricotta cheese, drained
1/4 grated Parmesan cheese
1/4 cup shredded mozzarella cheese
16 ounces pasta dough

1 egg, lightly beaten with
   1 tablespoon water, for sealing
   ravioli

With an electric mixer, beat ricotta cheese until smooth. Blend in Parmesan and mozzarella cheeses. Cover and refrigerate 30 minutes. (Filling may be prepared in advance and refrigerated up to 2 days.)

Roll and fill the pasta, as directed on pages 122–123.

When sauce is ready, cook ravioli in boiling water in a very large stockpot 7 minutes (10 to 12 minutes, if frozen).

Drain cooked ravioli.

Puttanesca Sauce

YIELD: *about 3 cups; 4 to 6 servings*

2 tablespoons extra-virgin olive oil
3 cloves garlic, minced
1 (28-ounce) can chopped tomatoes
6 oil-packed anchovies, chopped
3 tablespoons capers
1/3 cup pitted green olives

1/3 cup pitted ripe olives such as
  kalamata
1/4 teaspoon hot pepper flakes
1/4 teaspoon freshly ground black
  pepper

Heat olive oil in a large skillet or saucepan over medium heat. Add garlic and sauté 1 minute to soften; do not brown. Add the tomatoes, anchovies, capers, green and ripe olives, hot pepper flakes, and black pepper. Bring to a boil, then reduce heat and simmer 15 minutes. Taste and adjust seasonings if necessary. (Sauce may be prepared in advance and refrigerated up to 2 days. Reheat over medium heat before serving.)

To serve, toss drained ravioli with sauce and serve immediately.

Artichoke-Heart Ravioli with Roasted Peppers and Herbs

This artichoke filling was inspired by a ubiquitous party dip—a combination of artichoke hearts, mayonnaise, and some kind of cheese—which appears in every other community cookbook. I am not a fan of mayonnaise, but this dip is addictive, and I thought a variation would make a great ravioli filling. I spruced it up with a combination of Parmesan and smoked Cheddar cheeses, which are complemented by the smokiness of the roasted peppers in the sauce. The parsley and mint add color and fresh flavor. This is a nice spring and summer pasta. Use plain, canned artichokes, not those marinated in oil.

Recommended pasta recipes: Roasted Red Pepper Pasta (page 24), Asparagus Pasta (page 32), Black Pepper Pasta (page 66).

Other recommended accompaniments: Asparagus-Mushroom Sauce (page 131); Roasted Red Pepper Sauce (page 25); Pesto (page 53).

Makes 4 to 6 servings.

Artichoke-Heart Ravioli

YIELD: *1 1/4 cups filling, enough for about 80 to 90 ravioli*

1 (14-ounce) can artichoke hearts, drained
1/4 cup mayonnaise
1/4 cup grated Parmesan cheese
1/4 cup shredded smoked Cheddar cheese

16 ounces pasta dough
1 egg, lightly beaten with 1 tablespoon water, for sealing ravioli

Drain artichoke hearts, rinse under cold water, and squeeze out any excess liquid. Cut artichoke hearts into quarters. With motor running, drop artichoke hearts through feed tube into the work bowl of a food processor and process until finely minced.

Transfer minced artichoke hearts to a medium bowl. Add mayonnaise and cheeses and beat 1 minute with an electric mixer or a wooden spoon. Cover and refrigerate 30 minutes. (Filling may be prepared in advance and refrigerated up to 2 days.)

Roll and fill the pasta, as directed on pages 122–123.

When bell pepper mixture is ready, cook ravioli in boiling water in a very large stockpot 7 minutes (10 to 12 minutes, if frozen).

Drain cooked ravioli.

Roasted Peppers and Herbs

YIELD: *6 servings*

1 large red bell pepper
1 large yellow bell pepper
1 large orange bell pepper
1 tablespoon extra-virgin olive oil
1 tablespoon fresh lemon juice
1/4 teaspoon salt

1/2 cup finely chopped fresh parsley
2 tablespoons finely chopped fresh mint
2 tablespoons finely chopped fresh basil

Roast or grill bell peppers according to directions on page 24. When the skins are black, remove from oven and let cool. When cool enough to handle, remove skins from the peppers. (Bell peppers may be prepared in advance up to this point and refrigerated overnight.) Cut bell peppers lengthwise into 1/4-inch-wide strips.

Heat oil in a medium skillet over medium heat. Add bell peppers and cook 2 to 3 minutes, just until heated through. Remove from heat and stir in lemon juice and salt.

Toss together parsley, mint, and basil; mix with bell peppers. Add cooked ravioli and stir together. Serve immediately.

Refried-Bean Ravioli with Spicy Cheddar Sauce

Traditional refried beans are fried with lots and lots of lard. I make them more healthful by using olive oil and reducing the amount of fat from 1/2 cup to 2 teaspoons, then adding other favorite ingredients. This is easy to make and very pleasing.

Spicy Cheddar Sauce starts out as a béchamel sauce, with cheese and salsa stirred in. Do not use skim milk in the sauce; it does not incorporate well. It tastes okay, but the texture is lumpy.

Recommended pasta recipes: Tomato Pasta (page 20), Cilantro Pasta (page 58), Black Pepper Pasta (page 66), Chips 'n' Salsa Pasta (page 76).

Other recommended accompaniments: Cilantro-Lime Pesto (page 59), Watercress, Fresh Mozzarella, and Lime Vinaigrette (page 45), Maquechou (page 83), Roasted Tomato and Corn Salsa (page 77).

Makes 4 to 6 servings.

Refried-Bean Ravioli

YIELD: *1 1/3 cups filling, enough for about 80 to 90 ravioli*

2 teaspoons olive oil
1 small onion, finely chopped
1 clove garlic
1 (15-ounce) can pinto beans,
   drained and rinsed (about
   1 1/2 cups cooked beans)
1/4 teaspoon ground cumin
1/8 teaspoon salt

2 tablespoons salsa
6 drops Tabasco sauce
1/2 cup shredded Cheddar cheese
16 ounces pasta dough
1 egg, lightly beaten with
   1 tablespoon water, for sealing
   ravioli

Heat olive oil in a medium skillet over medium heat. Add onion and sauté until onion begins to soften, about 5 minutes. Add garlic and cook until onion is translucent, about 10 minutes. Add beans and mix with onion. Stir in cumin and cook 2 to 3 minutes, just to warm beans.

Transfer beans to a bowl and mash using a potato ricer or food mill. Add salt, salsa, and Tabasco sauce and mix thoroughly; cool. Add Cheddar cheese and stir just to mix. (Filling may be prepared in advance and refrigerated up to 2 days.)

Roll and fill the pasta, as directed on pages 122–123.

When sauce is ready, cook ravioli in boiling water in a very large stockpot 7 minutes (10 to 12 minutes, if frozen).

Drain cooked ravioli.

Spicy Cheddar Sauce

YIELD: *2 cups; 4 to 6 servings*

3 tablespoons butter
3 tablespoons all-purpose flour
About 2 cups whole milk
1 cup shredded Cheddar cheese
About 1/2 cup prepared salsa, at room
    temperature

1/4 teaspoon salt
1/4 cup chopped fresh cilantro, for
    garnish

Melt butter in a small saucepan over medium-low heat. Gradually add flour, stirring constantly. Cook, stirring, 2 minutes, then remove from heat.

Heat 2 cups milk in another small saucepan until hot to the touch or cook in a microwave-safe dish on HIGH 3 minutes. Pour hot milk into the flour mixture and whisk to blend.

Return sauce to medium-high heat and bring to a boil, stirring constantly. Reduce heat and simmer 2 to 3 minutes or until sauce thickens to the consistency of pancake batter. Reduce heat to low and stir in cheese. Cook, stirring, until cheese melts. Stir in salsa and salt and cook over low heat until warm. Set aside. To ensure that a skin does not form on the surface, pour a few tablespoons of milk over the surface.

To serve, divide drained ravioli among 4 to 6 individual plates. If sauce seems too thick, stir in additional salsa and ladle sauce on each serving. Garnish with chopped cilantro.

Lasagne with Spinach and Mushrooms

Lasagne can be a production, but always worth the effort. It is a substantial dish that can be prepared in advance, frozen, and reheated. There are a few steps needed to make this version, but once everything is done, you simply assemble and bake. All the separate parts—the tomato sauce, the béchamel sauce, the mushrooms, the spinach, and the pasta—can be prepared in advance. The actual assembly takes about 15 minutes. The result is an attractive, delectable dish.

Use this recipe as a model for creating your own lasagne recipe. Lasagne is very forgiving.

Recommended pasta recipes: Spinach Pasta (page 18), Roasted Red Pepper Pasta (page 24), Mushroom Pasta (page 38), Caramelized-Onion Pasta (page 34), Roasted Garlic Pasta (page 36).

Lasagne

Makes 12 servings.

1 tablespoon butter
1 medium onion, minced
1/4 teaspoon salt
1/8 teaspoon freshly ground black
    pepper
1 1/2 pounds mushrooms, stems
    trimmed and caps cut into
    thin slices
1 recipe Béchamel Sauce (see opposite)
1 recipe Chunky Tomato Sauce
    (page 171)
1 (10-ounce) package frozen spinach,
    thawed and cooked according
    to package instructions, excess
    liquid squeezed out

1/2 pound mozzarella cheese, shredded
16 ounces pasta dough, cut into
    12 to 14 pieces and rolled thin
    according to directions on
    page 124

BÉCHAMEL SAUCE
3 tablespoons unsalted butter
3 tablespoons all-purpose flour
2 cups milk, plus 2 or 3 tablespoons
1/4 teaspoon salt
1/8 teaspoon freshly ground black
    pepper
1/8 teaspoon freshly grated nutmeg

Melt butter in a large skillet or saucepan over medium heat. Add onion and cook until translucent, about 5 to 8 minutes.

Sprinkle salt and pepper over onion, then add mushrooms and stir. Cook over medium-high heat until mushrooms begin releasing their juices, about 12 to 15 minutes, stirring occasionally. Cook until juices have almost evaporated, 10 to 12 minutes. Remove from heat and set aside.

Make Béchamel Sauce: Melt butter in a small saucepan over medium-low heat. Sprinkle in the flour, stirring constantly. Cook, stirring constantly, 2 minutes, then remove from heat.

Heat 2 cups milk in another small saucepan until hot to the touch or cook in a microwave-safe dish on HIGH 3 minutes. Gradually pour hot milk into the flour mixture and whisk to blend.

Return sauce to medium-high heat and bring to a boil, stirring constantly. Reduce heat and simmer 2 to 3 minutes or until sauce thickens to the consistency of pancake batter. Remove from heat and stir in salt, pepper, and nutmeg; set aside. To ensure that a skin does not form on the surface, pour a few tablespoons of milk over the surface.

To make in advance, let cool slightly, then cover the surface directly with a sheet of waxed paper so a skin will not form and refrigerate up to 1 day. Makes 1 3/4 cups.

Have mushrooms, Béchamel Sauce, tomato sauce, spinach, and cheese ready before you cook the pasta.

Preheat oven to 350F (175C) and lightly grease a 13 x 9-inch baking pan.

Cook 4 sheets of pasta at a time in boiling, salted water about 3 minutes or just until barely cooked. Rinse the first batch under cold water and start assembling lasagne while the next batch cooks.

Assemble the lasagne: Spoon about 1/2 cup tomato sauce over the bottom of the prepared pan. Place cooked lasagne sheets over the bottom of pan, overlapping slightly so that there are no gaps. Spread 1/4 of the Béchamel Sauce over the pasta. Sprinkle 1/3 of the mushrooms on top of the Béchamel Sauce, then add 1/3 of the tomato sauce, followed by 1/3 of the spinach in small spoonfuls at intervals across the surface, then 1/4 of the mozzarella cheese. It's easiest to spread all these layers with your hands.

Top the mozzarella with another layer of pasta, followed by another 1/4 of the Béchamel Sauce, 1/3 of the mushrooms, 1/3 of the tomato sauce, 1/3 of the spinach, and 1/4 of the mozzarella cheese. Repeat again with another layer, and end with a fourth layer of pasta. Top this with the remaining Béchamel Sauce and mozzarella cheese. There should be at least 1/2 inch of space between the top layer of pasta and the top of the pan; use a spatula to press down and flatten slightly, if necessary. Cover pan with foil. (The lasagne may be prepared in advance at this point and refrigerated overnight.)

Bake at 350F (175C) 45 minutes (60 minutes, if the lasagne has been refrigerated overnight). Remove foil and bake 15 to 20 minutes, until the top is golden brown. Let stand 5 minutes, then serve. Refrigerate any remaining lasagne for great leftovers.

Sloppy Joe Lasagne

This lasagne is simpler than the above recipe, as it has only one element to layer between the pasta—the Sloppy Joe Sauce. A real family favorite, this recipe seems to appeal to all ages; both my sons, who have radically different tastes in food, ask for seconds. Parents and grandparents enjoy it, too. The sauce can be prepared the day before, and assembly takes about 15 minutes.

Recommended pasta recipes: Tomato Pasta (page 20), Roasted Garlic Pasta (page 36), Beer-Paprika Pasta (page 114).

Makes 12 servings.

Sloppy Joe Lasagne

Sloppy Joe Sauce (see below)
1 teaspoon olive oil
1/2 cup bread crumbs
16 ounces pasta dough, cut into
    12 to 14 pieces and rolled
    according to directions on
    page 124

SLOPPY JOE SAUCE
1 pound ground beef
1 large onion, finely chopped
2 medium carrots, grated

1 green bell pepper, diced
1 yellow bell pepper, diced
1 (28-ounce) can tomato puree
2 (6-ounce) cans tomato paste
1 tablespoon Worcestershire sauce
1 tablespoon cider vinegar
2 tablespoons honey
2 tablespoons molasses
1 teaspoon chili powder
3/4 teaspoon salt
1/4 teaspoon freshly ground black
    pepper

Prepare Sloppy Joe Sauce: Crumble ground beef into a large pot and sauté over medium-high heat. After about 3 minutes, add onion. Cook 3 minutes, stirring occasionally to break up beef, then add carrots and bell peppers. Cook until beef is thoroughly browned and onion is translucent, about 10 minutes.

While meat is cooking, mix together tomato puree and tomato paste in a bowl. Add Worcestershire sauce, cider vinegar, honey, molasses, chili powder, salt, and black pepper and mix thoroughly. Add to ground beef mixture and stir to combine. Bring to a boil over medium-high heat, then reduce heat, cover, and simmer 15 minutes, until bell peppers are tender. Remove lid and simmer 5 minutes. (Sauce may be prepared in advance and kept refrigerated overnight.) Makes 7 cups.

Preheat oven to 350F (175C) and lightly grease a 13 x 9-inch baking pan. Mix olive oil with bread crumbs and set aside.

Cook 4 sheets of pasta at a time in boiling, salted water about 3 minutes or just until barely cooked. Rinse the first batch under cold water and start assembling lasagne while the next batch cooks.

To assemble: Spoon about 1/2 cup sauce over the bottom of prepared pan. Place the cooked lasagne sheets over the bottom of pan, overlapping slightly so that there are no gaps. Spread 2 cups of sauce over the pasta. Cover with another layer of pasta, another 2 cups of sauce, pasta, 2 cups of sauce, then pasta. There should be 1/2 cup of sauce remaining. Spread this over the top layer of the pasta, then sprinkle with the reserved bread crumbs. There should be at least 1/2 inch of space between the top layer of pasta and the top of the pan; use a spatula to press down and flatten slightly, if necessary. Cover pan with foil. (Lasagne may be prepared in advance up to this point and refrigerated overnight.)

Bake 45 minutes (or 60 minutes, if the lasagne has been refrigerated overnight). Remove foil and bake 15 to 20 minutes, until the bread crumbs have begun to turn golden brown. Let stand 5 to 10 minutes, then serve. Refrigerate any remaining lasagne for great leftovers.

Apple-Apple Kugel

Kugel is a traditional Jewish noodle pudding, rich with eggs, butter, and sour cream. Occasionally it calls for fruit, both fresh and dried. I always liked apple kugel, which tastes like a cross between apple pie, pudding, and bread pudding. It tastes that much better when made with the Apple Pasta (page 40). Several variations are also offered.

YIELD: *16 servings*

4 eggs
1/3 cup packed light brown sugar
1/8 teaspoon salt
1/2 cup cottage cheese
1/2 cup sour cream
16 ounces Apple Pasta (page 40),
    cut into fettuccine noodles

3 tablespoons butter
4 apples, peeled, cored, coarsely
    grated (about 5 cups), and
    tossed with 2 tablespoons
    lemon juice to prevent
    discoloration

Preheat oven to 350F (175C). Butter a 13 x 9-inch pan.

Using an electric mixer on medium speed, beat together eggs, brown sugar, and salt until well blended, about 3 minutes. Add cottage cheese and sour cream and beat 1 minute.

Cook the pasta in boiling water until just tender to the bite, about 2 to 3 minutes. Drain, turn pasta into large bowl, and immediately toss with 2 tablespoons of the butter until butter melts and coats the pasta. Stir in grated apples.

Pour egg mixture into the noodle mixture and stir to mix thoroughly. Pour into prepared pan. Cut remaining tablespoon of butter into small pieces and dot surface of casserole with butter.

Bake 55 to 60 minutes or until the top begins to brown. Serve warm or cold.

Variations

Cinnamon-Apple Kugel   Add 1/2 teaspoon ground cinnamon to the dry ingredients when making the pasta. Add 1/2 teaspoon ground cinnamon to the egg-and-sour-cream mixture.

Cranberry, Nut, and Apple Kugel Use Cranberry Pasta (page 114) instead of Apple Pasta. Add 1/2 cup chopped walnuts and 1/2 cup dried fruit such as dried cranberries or raisins with the apples.

Crunchy-Top Apple Kugel Melt remaining 1 tablespoon butter and toss with 2 cups corn flakes and 1 tablespoon brown sugar. Sprinkle over kugel and bake as directed.

Gnocchi

Gnocchi are quite different from the pastas in the rest of this book. Literally, *gnocchi* means "dumpling," and these are thick, curved dumplings with ridges on one side to help hold the sauce. (All the machines I tested come with a gnocchi die.) Whereas other pastas have a relatively high ratio of flour to liquid, with gnocchi, that ratio is closer to fifty/fifty. For other pastas, the desired texture of pasta-machine dough is crumbly, with bits of dough the size of peas and walnuts. For gnocchi, the dough should come together as a ball and have more or less the texture of bread or pie crust dough—easy to roll between the palms of your hands and slightly sticky if you press it firmly between your fingers.

Types of Gnocchi

There are two standard types of Italian gnocchi: potato and ricotta. Potato gnocchi are best made with russet potatoes, which are drier than new potatoes. Michele

Topor, who teaches Italian cooking classes in Boston, recommends baking the potatoes rather than boiling them, as it makes the potato drier still. The object is to use a minimal amount of flour. Lilly d'Alelio, a professional pasta maker, makes gnocchi in such large quantities that boiling is the only viable option. But she recommends using older potatoes, potatoes that have sat through a winter of cold storage, for example. She feels they yield more flavorful gnocchi.

There are different schools of thought as to whether or not potato gnocchi should have eggs or not. Marcella Hazan in *The Essentials of Classic Italian Cooking* (Knopf, 1992) disparages the idea of using eggs, unless your gnocchi absolutely won't hold their shape during cooking. Biba Caggiano, in *Trattoria Cooking* (Macmillan, 1992) gives instructions for gnocchi with eggs, but does comment that eggless gnocchi are indeed lighter. I include recipes for both types; you be the judge.

Ricotta cheese–based gnocchi are also traditional, and their flavor and texture are somewhat different from those of potato gnocchi. I tested the recipes in this chapter using both whole milk and part-skim ricotta, and both worked well.

Other vegetables, such as sweet potatoes, may also be used for gnocchi. Sweet potatoes are moister than regular potatoes; I found white sweet potatoes to be a little drier than yellow sweet potatoes. Because sweet potatoes are so moist, however, I made these gnocchi without eggs, as the version with eggs required so much flour that they tasted unappealingly tough and chewy.

Making Gnocchi in the Pasta Machine

Gnocchi are very quick to mix in the pasta machine. The key is not to overmix. Unlike with regular pasta, the gluten in the flour should not be overdeveloped, which is caused by excessive kneading. That chewy texture from the gluten is undesirable in thick gnocchi. For this reason, a lower-protein flour is best. Semolina and durum flours are higher in protein and therefore less preferable for gnocchi. The following recipes were all made with regular all-purpose flour. You can also experiment with different kinds of flours such as whole wheat.

The trick to making gnocchi in a pasta machine is not to overprocess the dough, which will yield tough, gummy gnocchi. Also, sometimes if the entire ball of dough is in the machine, the corkscrew will keep picking up the dough as it tries to go into the extruder, and nothing will extrude. For these reasons, I recommend using a technique similar to that used for breadsticks and pretzels in the "Not Just Pasta" chapter.

Extruding Gnocchi

Once the dough is mixed, remove it from the machine. Tear off pieces of dough and press them into the extruding portion of your machine. Turn the machine on; as the dough spirals down the corkscrew, turn the machine off and press more dough into the extruder. The gnocchi will start to come out. Cut the dough every inch, stopping the machine on occasion to add more dough to the extruder.

This technique serves two purposes. First, it ensures that the dough goes through the extruder and doesn't just twirl around in the machine bowl. But second, and more important, it minimizes the amount of kneading the dough receives. The more gnocchi are kneaded, the tougher their texture. Kneading also makes the dough moister, requiring more flour, again at the expense of flavor and texture.

Cooking Gnocchi

Ultimately, gnocchi are very quick to make. The dough mixes and extrudes quickly, and it cooks very rapidly as well. It is best to cook gnocchi in small batches of about one-half pound each to ensure that they aren't overcooked. Ricotta gnocchi tend to cook faster than potato gnocchi. Both cook in 1 to 4 minutes.

To cook gnocchi, drop into a large pot of boiling water. When the gnocchi rise to the surface, cook another 10 to 20 seconds, then remove immediately and mix with sauce, as instructed in the recipes.

Storing Gnocchi

Gnocchi may be refrigerated up to two days. It is best to store them in one layer, covered with plastic wrap. To freeze, place plate with single layer of gnocchi in freezer. Let freeze until firm, several hours. When firm, put gnocchi in a plastic bag and seal. You can cook frozen gnocchi directly from the freezer, although they will take a few minutes longer to cook than fresh gnocchi.

Basic Potato Gnocchi with Gorgonzola Sauce

Potatoes always go well with dairy products such as cheese, cream, and butter, and potato gnocchi are no exception. A classic accompaniment for gnocchi is Gorgonzola sauce; the saltiness of this Italian cheese goes perfectly with the gnocchi. If you can find Gorgonzola dolce, also called Docelatte cheese, use it; it is softer and creamier than the aged, more crumbly Gorgonzola, although regular Gorgonzola works just fine. Other blue cheeses, such as creamy Saga Blue cheese or Roquefort, may also be used. This is a very rich dish, and the servings are a little smaller than they might be for other pastas. I like to add color to the potatoes with the addition of steamed, chopped spinach or green peas.

Traditionally, the sauce is made with cream, which on top of the butter and creamy cheese I find way too rich. I make it with whole milk, and it is delicious.

Other recommended accompaniments: Cucumber Sauce (page 51), Garlicky Chili con Carne (page 120), Roasted Garlic Sauce and Peas (page 37), Mushroom-Herb Pesto (page 39).

Makes 6 servings.

Basic Potato Gnocchi

YIELD: *20 ounces*

1 1/2 pounds russet potatoes (about 2 large or 4 medium), rinsed and dried

1 large egg, lightly beaten
1/2 teaspoon salt
1 1/2 to 2 cups all-purpose flour

Bake potatoes: Preheat oven to 425F (220C). Place potatoes directly on oven rack. Bake 25 minutes. Open oven and pierce each potato with a fork to allow steam to escape. Bake until easily pierced with a fork, about 1 hour total for large potatoes, 45 minutes total for medium.

Remove potatoes from oven and allow to cool until you can handle them easily. Scoop flesh from the skins into a bowl and mash with a potato masher or fork. Do not puree; pureeing releases the potato starch and makes the potatoes gummy. You should have about 1 1/2 to 1 3/4 cups mashed potatoes. (The potatoes may be baked in advance and refrigerated for up to 3 days. Allow to come to room temperature before mashing.)

Place mashed potatoes in the bowl of the pasta machine. Mix about 1 minute, then add the egg with machine running and mix until incorporated.

Turn off machine and sprinkle in the salt and 1 1/2 cups flour. Turn the machine on and mix until the flour is blended with the potatoes, about 1 minute. The dough should be pliable, easy to roll between the palms of your hand, yet sticky if you squeeze it. If it feels too sticky, add additional flour, 2 tablespoons at a time.

Once the dough is mixed, remove it from the machine. Tear off pieces of dough and press them into the extruding portion of your machine. Turn the machine on. As the dough spirals down the corkscrew, turn the machine off and press more dough into the extruder. The gnocchi will start to come out. Sprinkle flour over the surface onto which you are extruding, and have a bowl with flour nearby.

Cut the dough every 1 inch. The gnocchi dough extrudes very quickly, so you will need to work fast. Sprinkle the extruded gnocchi with flour to prevent sticking. Keep the gnocchi in one layer; do not let them pile up as you might with other pasta. They will stick and turn from a pile of gnocchi back into a lump of dough.

When sauce is ready, cook gnocchi in batches in boiling salted water until they rise to the surface of the water, about 1 to 3 minutes, and then cook 10 to 20 seconds longer. Drain, mix with sauce, and serve immediately.

Gorgonzola Sauce

YIELD: *6 servings*

2 tablespoons unsalted butter
4 ounces Gorgonzola cheese, cut
    into 1/2-inch pieces
1/4 cup milk

1/8 teaspoon freshly ground black
    pepper
1/8 teaspoon salt

Melt butter in a large saucepan over medium heat. Add Gorgonzola cheese and stir constantly as cheese melts, mixing it into the butter. Slowly pour in the milk and cook, stirring constantly, until smooth and creamy. Add salt and pepper and use immediately. To serve, mix gnocchi with sauce in the saucepan, then divide among individual plates.

Eggless Potato Gnocchi with Browned Butter Sauce

Most gnocchi recipes include eggs; they help the gnocchi stay together better and they are easier to work with. But I find the eggless gnocchi have a stronger potato taste than the version with eggs, although both are delicious. It's worth trying each to see what fits your taste. The key here is not to overcook the gnocchi. When overcooked, they tend to become mushy when you add them to the browned butter.

Other recommended accompaniments: Beef 'n' Beer Goulash (page 115), Herb-Roasted Vegetables (page 49), Pesto (page 53), Walnut–Goat Cheese Sauce (page 35).

Makes 4 servings.

Eggless Potato Gnocchi

YIELD: *18 ounces*

1 1/2 pounds russet potatoes (about 2 large or 4 medium), rinsed and dried

1/4 teaspoon salt
3/4 to 1 cup all-purpose flour

Bake potatoes and mash as directed on page 154.

Place mashed potatoes in the bowl of the pasta machine. Mix about 1 minute, then add salt and mix 30 seconds.

Turn off machine and sprinkle in 3/4 cup flour. Turn the machine on and mix until the flour is blended with the potatoes, about 1 minute. The dough should be pliable, easy to roll between the palms of your hand, yet sticky if you squeeze it. If it feels too sticky, add additional flour, 2 tablespoons at a time.

Once the dough is mixed, remove it from the machine. Tear off pieces of dough and press them into the extruding portion of your machine. Turn the machine on. As the dough spirals down the corkscrew, turn the machine off and press more dough into the extruder. The gnocchi will start to come out. Sprinkle flour over the surface onto which you are extruding, and have a bowl with flour nearby.

Cut the dough every 1 inch. The gnocchi dough extrudes very quickly, so you will need to work fast. Sprinkle the extruded gnocchi with flour to prevent sticking. Keep the gnocchi in one layer; do not let them pile up as you might with other pasta. They will stick and turn from a pile of gnocchi back into a lump of dough.

When sauce is ready, cook gnocchi in batches in boiling salted water until they rise to the surface of the water, about 1 to 3 minutes, and then cook 10 to 20 seconds longer. Drain, mix with sauce, and serve immediately.

Browned Butter Sauce

YIELD: *2 tablespoons; 4 servings*

2 tablespoons lightly salted butter
4 teaspoons minced fresh parsley,
       for garnish

Melt butter in a large saucepan over medium-high heat. Cook until butter begins to brown, about 2 minutes. The water in the butter will boil out and the remaining liquid will be a dark nutty brown. Keep butter warm over very low heat until the gnocchi are cooked.

Add drained gnocchi to browned butter. Toss gently to coat thoroughly. Sprinkle each serving with a teaspoon of minced parsley.

Vichyssoise Gnocchi with Creamed Leeks

Vichyssoise is the classic French leek-and-potato soup, simple flavors that are so delicious. I wanted to transform this potato favorite into gnocchi. The accompanying leek sauce has a slight, pleasing tang from sour cream. This is a rich dish, and can serve four as an entrée or six as an appetizer.

Other recommended accompaniments: Asparagus-Mushroom Sauce (page 131), Cucumber Sauce (page 51), Smoked Trout Sauce (page 61).

Makes 4 to 6 servings.

Vichyssoise Gnocchi

YIELD: *18 ounces*

1 1/2 pounds russet potatoes (about 2 large or 4 medium), rinsed and dried
4 large leeks

2 tablespoons unsalted butter
3/4 teaspoon salt
1 to 1 1/4 cups all-purpose flour

Bake potatoes and mash as directed on page 154.

While potatoes are baking, prepare leeks. Cut each leek in half lengthwise, then cut each half into quarters lengthwise. Thinly slice white and pale green parts only. Rinse well and drain thoroughly.

Melt butter in a large skillet or saucepan over medium heat. Add leeks and stir. Cook about 5 minutes, until leeks begin to soften. Stir to mix with butter, cover, and cook over medium heat 8 to 10 minutes, until leeks are soft. Uncover and cook 5 minutes or until translucent and very soft. Let cool and measure 1/2 cup leeks. Add 1/2 cup leeks to the mashed potatoes and reserve the remaining leeks in skillet for sauce.

Place mashed potatoes and leeks in the bowl of the pasta machine. Run the machine for about 1 minute, then add the salt and mix for another 30 seconds.

Turn off machine and sprinkle in 1 cup flour. Turn the machine on and mix until the flour is blended with the potatoes, about 1 minute. The dough should be pliable, easy to roll between the palms of your hand, yet sticky if you squeeze it. If it feels too sticky, add additional flour, 2 tablespoons at a time.

Once the dough is mixed, remove it from the machine. Tear off pieces of dough and press them into the extruding portion of your machine. Turn the machine on. As the dough spirals down the corkscrew, turn the machine off and press more dough into the extruder. The gnocchi will start to come out. Sprinkle flour over the surface onto which you are extruding, and have a bowl with flour nearby.

Cut the dough every 1 inch. The gnocchi dough extrudes very quickly, so you will need to work fast. Sprinkle the extruded gnocchi with flour to prevent sticking. Keep the gnocchi in one layer; do not let them pile up as you might with other pasta. They will stick and turn from a pile of gnocchi back into a lump of dough.

When sauce is ready, cook gnocchi in batches in boiling salted water until they rise to the surface of the water, about 1 to 3 minutes, and then cook 10 to 20 seconds longer. Drain, mix with sauce, and serve immediately.

Creamed Leeks

YIELD: *1 1/2 cups; 6 servings*

1/2 cup sour cream
3/4 cup milk
Reserved cooked leeks (from above)
1/4 teaspoon salt

1/4 teaspoon freshly ground black
   pepper
2 tablespoons chopped chives

Whisk together sour cream and 1/4 cup of the milk, then add to leeks in skillet. Cook over medium heat. Mixture will curdle, but don't panic. Bring to a boil, then simmer to let it thicken and come together. Stir in salt and pepper, then transfer to a blender. Blend until pureed and thick. Add remaining 1/2 cup milk and blend until combined.

To serve, divide gnocchi among 4 to 6 plates and spoon sauce over each serving, tossing gently to coat. Sprinkle with chopped chives and serve immediately.

Samosa Gnocchi with Mango Chutney Sauce

One of my favorite potato preparations is the Indian appetizer samosa. *Samosas are triangular pastries most commonly filled with a spiced potato mixture and served with some kind of chutney. The pastry is most often made with regular flour, but sometimes includes chickpea flour, so I combined the two here. Chickpea flour, also called* besan, *is available from Indian markets or by mail (see "Sources," pages 197–198). If you are unable to find it, use an equal amount of all-purpose flour instead.*

This recipe works best with underripe mangos; as mangos ripen they get stringy, juicy, and difficult to cut into cubes.

Other recommended accompaniments: Cilantro-Lime Pesto (page 59), Indian Karhi Sauce and Chickpeas (page 87), Lemon-Ginger Sauce (page 128).

Makes 6 to 8 servings.

Samosa Gnocchi

YIELD: *28 ounces*

1 1/2 pounds russet potatoes (about 2 large or 4 medium), rinsed and dried
1 large onion, unpeeled, but ends trimmed and halved crosswise
1 tablespoon unsalted butter
1 clove garlic, minced

2 tablespoons grated ginger root
1 teaspoon mustard seeds
1 teaspoon ground coriander
2 tablespoons fresh lemon juice
1 teaspoon salt
1 cup chickpea flour
1 to 1 1/2 cups all-purpose flour

Bake potatoes and mash as directed on page 154. Bake onion with potatoes: Line a small pan with foil and lightly oil foil. Place onion, cut side down, in pan. Bake 25 to 30 minutes or until a knife slips in easily and bottom of onion is slightly brown.

Peel onion; cut each half into quarters. Process onion in a food processor until the texture of finely minced onion. There should be about 1/2 cup onion.

Melt butter in a small saucepan over medium heat. Add garlic and sauté 1 minute. Add ginger, mustard seeds, and coriander and cook 1 to 2 minutes or until mustard seeds begin to pop. Remove from heat, stir in lemon juice, and set aside.

Place mashed potatoes, minced onion, and butter mixture in the bowl of the pasta machine. Mix until blended, about 2 minutes. In a separate bowl, stir together the salt and the flours. With machine off, sprinkle flour mixture over the potatoes. Mix until the flours are blended with the potatoes, about 3 minutes. The dough should be pliable, easy to roll between the palms of your hands, yet sticky if you squeeze it. If it feels too sticky, add additional flour, 2 tablespoons at a time.

Once the dough is mixed, remove it from the machine. Tear off pieces of dough and press them into the extruding portion of your machine. Turn the machine on. As the dough spirals down the corkscrew, turn the machine off and press more dough into the extruder. The gnocchi will start to come out. Sprinkle flour over the surface onto which you are extruding, and have a bowl with flour nearby.

Cut the dough every 1 inch. The gnocchi dough extrudes very quickly, so you will need to work fast. Sprinkle the extruded gnocchi with flour to prevent sticking. Keep the gnocchi in one layer; do not let them pile up as you might with other pasta. They will stick and turn from a pile of gnocchi back into a lump of dough.

When sauce is ready, cook gnocchi in batches in boiling salted water until they rise to the surface of the water, about 1 to 3 minutes, and then cook 10 to 20 seconds longer. Drain, mix with sauce, and serve immediately.

Mango Chutney Sauce

YIELD: *1 1/2 cups; 6 to 8 servings*

1 mango, peeled, pitted, and
    chopped
1 medium onion, minced
1 tablespoon grated ginger root
1 clove garlic, minced
Zest of 1/2 lemon, cut into 1/4-inch
    pieces

1/4 cup fresh lemon juice
1/4 cup cider vinegar
1/2 cup packed dark brown sugar
1/3 cup raisins
1/8 teaspoon salt
1/2 cup orange juice
Orange wedges, for garnish

Combine mango, onion, ginger, garlic, lemon zest, lemon juice, vinegar, brown sugar, raisins, and salt in a medium saucepan. Bring to a boil over high heat, stirring to mix all ingredients. Reduce heat to low and simmer until onion is tender, about 20 to 30 minutes, stirring frequently as liquid evaporates and mixture thickens. The chutney should be the texture of thick honey. Stir in orange juice and heat over low heat just until warmed through. Toss with gnocchi and serve immediately, garnished with oranges.

Chestnut Gnocchi with Beurre Rouge

Chestnut flour, available in Italian markets or by mail (see "Sources," pages 197–198), has a slightly sweet, smoky flavor. When mixed with potatoes, as in this recipe, the chestnut flavor comes through distinctively. The natural sweetness of the chestnuts makes the dough slightly sticky, and the egg helps the gnocchi hold their shape. Chestnut gnocchi cook very quickly, usually in less than 1 minute, so watch them carefully.

The Beurre Rouge (red wine sauce) should be prepared just before you cook the gnocchi. It comes together as a smooth, creamy sauce, but if it sits for too long, the oil from the butter will separate. It has a meaty flavor, and indeed, this pasta goes well as a side to roast beef, steak, or other red-meat dishes. Serve with steamed broccoli, for a balance of textures and colors.

Other recommended accompaniments: Chestnut-Mushroom Delight (page 85), Green Bean–Red Onion Sauce (page 55), Herb-Roasted Vegetables (page 49), Walnut–Goat Cheese Sauce (page 35).

Makes 4 servings.

Chestnut Gnocchi

YIELD: *18 ounces*

1 1/2 pounds russet potatoes (about 2 large or 4 medium), rinsed and dried
1 egg, lightly beaten

1 cup chestnut flour
1/4 teaspoon salt
1/2 to 3/4 cup all-purpose flour

Bake potatoes and mash as directed on page 154.

Place mashed potatoes in the bowl of the pasta machine. Mix about 1 minute, then add egg with machine running and mix until incorporated.

Turn off machine and sprinkle in salt, chestnut flour, and 1/2 cup all-purpose flour. Turn the machine on and mix until the flours are blended with the potatoes, about 1 minute. The dough should be pliable, easy to roll between the palms of your hand, yet sticky if you squeeze it. If it feels too sticky, add additional flour, 2 tablespoons at a time.

Once the dough is mixed, remove it from the machine. Tear off pieces of dough and press them into the extruding portion of your machine. Turn the machine on. As the dough spirals down the corkscrew, turn the machine off and press more dough into the extruder. The gnocchi will start to come out. Sprinkle flour over the surface onto which you are extruding, and have a bowl with flour nearby.

Cut the dough every 1 inch. The gnocchi dough extrudes very quickly, so you will need to work fast. Sprinkle the extruded gnocchi with flour to prevent sticking. Keep the gnocchi in one layer; do not let them pile up as you might with other pasta. They will stick and turn from a pile of gnocchi back into a lump of dough.

When sauce is ready, cook gnocchi in batches in boiling salted water until they rise to the surface of the water, about 1 to 3 minutes, and then cook 10 to 20 seconds longer. Drain, mix with sauce, and serve immediately.

Beurre Rouge

YIELD: *scant 1/2 cup; 4 servings*

1/2 cup red wine
1/4 cup finely minced red onion
1/4 teaspoon salt
1/8 teaspoon freshly ground black
   pepper

6 tablespoons unsalted butter, cut
   into 12 pieces

Combine wine, onion, salt, and pepper in a small saucepan. Bring to a boil over high heat, then simmer until reduced to about 2 tablespoons of liquid, about 3 to 4 minutes. Reduce heat to very low and immediately stir in 2 pieces of butter. When butter is melted and incorporated into the wine, stir in 2 more pieces. Continue adding butter and stirring until incorporated until all the butter has been used. The sauce should be a rich maroon color. Keep warm over very low heat. As soon as the gnocchi are cooked, toss with the sauce and serve immediately.

Jerusalem Artichoke Gnocchi with Balsamic Vinaigrette, Watercress, and Mushrooms

Jerusalem artichokes, also called sunchokes, actually have nothing to do with either Jerusalem or artichokes. In fact, they are roots of sunflowers, gerisole in French, which somehow got transformed into Jerusalem when translated into English. The taste, vaguely reminiscent of artichokes, is distinctive and delicious, and pairs very well with potatoes. These small, knobby tubers are much moister, however, than potatoes, and they require more flour. For this reason, I make these gnocchi without eggs; otherwise the gnocchi would require so much flour that the flavor would be lost.

Note that the Jerusalem artichokes need to be pureed or they will be too lumpy and make extruding difficult. Do not, however, puree the potatoes.

Other recommended accompaniments: Asparagus, Leeks, and Red Peppers (page 33), Lamb and Chickpea Stew (page 117), Roasted Garlic Sauce and Peas (page 37), Rosy Vegetable Sauce (page 27).

Makes 4 servings.

Jerusalem Artichoke Gnocchi

YIELD: *16 ounces*

3/4 pound russet potatoes (about 1 large or 2 medium), rinsed and dried	3/4 pound Jerusalem artichokes 1/2 teaspoon salt 2 cups all-purpose flour

Bake potatoes and mash as directed on page 154.

While the potatoes are baking, cook Jerusalem artichokes: Bring a large pot of water to a boil. While the water is heating, peel artichokes and slice into 1/4-inch-thick slices. Add artichokes to boiling water and cook until tender, about 15 to 20 minutes. Remove with a slotted spoon and drain on paper towels. Let stand until cool.

Process artichokes in a food processor or food mill until pureed. Combine pureed artichokes and mashed potatoes in the bowl of the pasta machine. Mix together 1 minute. Add salt and mix 1 minute to combine the ingredients.

Turn off machine and sprinkle in 1 1/2 cups flour. Turn the machine on and mix until the flour is blended with the potatoes, about 1 minute. The dough should be pliable, easy to roll between the palms of your hands, yet sticky if you squeeze it. If it feels too sticky, add additional flour, 2 tablespoons at a time.

Once the dough is mixed, remove it from the machine. Tear off pieces of dough and press them into the extruding portion of your machine. Turn the machine on. As the dough spirals down the corkscrew, turn the machine off and press more dough into the extruder. The gnocchi will start to come out. Sprinkle flour over the surface onto which you are extruding, and have a bowl with flour nearby.

Cut the dough every 1 inch. The gnocchi dough extrudes very quickly, so you will need to work fast. Sprinkle the extruded gnocchi with flour to prevent sticking. Keep the gnocchi in one layer; do not let them pile up as you might with other pasta. They will stick and turn from a pile of gnocchi back into a lump of dough.

When vinaigrette is ready, cook gnocchi in batches in boiling salted water until they rise to the surface of the water, about 1 to 3 minutes, and then cook 10 to 20 seconds longer. Drain, mix with vinaigrette, and serve immediately.

Balsamic Vinaigrette, Watercress, and Mushrooms

YIELD: *4 servings*

1/2 teaspoon salt
1/4 teaspoon freshly ground black
  pepper
3 tablespoons balsamic vinegar
1/4 cup olive oil
2 bunches watercress, washed and
  thick stems removed

1/2 pound mushrooms, stems
  trimmed, cleaned, cut in half,
  and then cut into 1/4-inch-
  thick slices
4 tablespoons grated Parmesan
  cheese

Whisk together salt, pepper, balsamic vinegar, and olive oil in a bowl until thoroughly combined. Toss drained gnocchi with 4 tablespoons vinaigrette.

To serve, divide the watercress among 4 plates, top with sliced mushrooms, and drizzle each serving with 1 1/2 teaspoons of dressing. Top each portion with equal amount of gnocchi and sprinkle with 1 tablespoon Parmesan cheese. Serve immediately.

Sweet Potato Gnocchi with Rosemary-Garlic Sauce

Sweet potatoes are moister than regular russet potatoes. I experimented with these gnocchi several times before devising a formula that works: I omitted the eggs. Eggs make the dough too wet, requiring too much flour, yielding a tougher dumpling. As with regular potato gnocchi, be careful not to overknead.

Sweet potato gnocchi are slightly heavier than gnocchi made with regular potatoes, but they have a wonderful flavor. I offer two sweet potato recipes. This one is with savory spices and flavorings; the following recipe accentuates the vegetable's natural sweetness. This recipe works well as an entrée or as a side to turkey or chicken.

Other recommended accompaniments: Edam Cheese Sauce (page 21), Honey-Lemon Chicken (page 111), Watercress, Fresh Mozzarella, and Lime Vinaigrette (page 45), Lime-Pistachio Sauce (page 133).

Makes 4 servings.

Sweet Potato Gnocchi

YIELD: *16 ounces*

1 pound sweet potatoes (about
    2 small or 1 large), rinsed and
    dried
1/4 teaspoon salt

1/2 teaspoon freshly ground black
    pepper
1/4 cup grated Parmesan cheese
1 to 1 1/4 cups all-purpose flour

Bake the sweet potatoes as for russet potatoes, page 154.

Remove potatoes from oven and allow to cool until you can handle them easily. Peel (the skins should slip off easily) and place flesh in a bowl. Mash with a potato masher or fork; do not puree. There should be just over 1 cup mashed sweet potatoes.

Place the mashed sweet potatoes in the bowl of the pasta machine. Mix about 1 minute, then add the salt, pepper and Parmesan cheese and mix 30 seconds.

Turn off machine and sprinkle in 1 cup flour. Turn the machine on and mix until the flour is blended with the potatoes, about 1 minute. The dough should be pliable, easy to roll between the palms of your hands, yet sticky if you squeeze it. If it feels too sticky, add additional flour, 2 tablespoons at a time.

Once the dough is mixed, remove it from the machine. Tear off pieces of dough and press them into the extruding portion of your machine. Turn the machine on. As the dough spirals down the corkscrew, turn the machine off and press more dough into the extruder. The gnocchi will start to come out. Sprinkle flour over the surface onto which you are extruding, and have a bowl with flour nearby.

Cut the dough every 1 inch. The gnocchi dough extrudes very quickly, so you will need to work fast. Sprinkle the extruded gnocchi with flour to prevent sticking. Keep the gnocchi in one layer; do not let them pile up as you might with other pasta. They will stick and turn from a pile of gnocchi back into a lump of dough.

When sauce is ready, cook gnocchi in batches in boiling salted water until they rise to the surface of the water, about 1 to 3 minutes, and then cook 10 to 20 seconds longer. Drain, mix with sauce, and serve immediately.

Rosemary-Garlic Sauce

YIELD: *4 servings*

3 tablespoons extra-virgin olive oil
3 cloves garlic, finely minced (about
    1 tablespoon)
1 teaspoon dried rosemary

1/4 teaspoon salt
1/4 teaspoon freshly ground black
    pepper

Heat olive oil in a large saucepan over medium-high heat. Add garlic and rosemary and sauté until garlic begins to turn golden. Immediately remove from heat; do not let garlic brown. Add salt and pepper and stir. Toss gnocchi with the oil, then heat 1 to 2 minutes. Serve immediately.

Spiced Sweet Potato Gnocchi with Sherried Apples and Pecans

Sweet potatoes are naturally sweet, and they tend to be prepared with brown sugar, marshmallows, and the like. Sweet spices—in this case allspice, ginger, and cardamom—bring out the natural sweetness of this tuber. This dish goes well with meats such as ham or roast pork.

The sauce should be prepared just before you are ready to cook the gnocchi.

Other recommended accompaniments: Maple-Walnut Sauce (page 93), Orange Butter Sauce (page 43), Pear Vinaigrette and Greens (page 137), Pumpkin-Cider Sauce (page 135).

Makes 4 servings.

Spiced Sweet Potato Gnocchi

YIELD: *16 ounces*

1 pound sweet potatoes (about
    2 small or 1 large)
1/2 teaspoon salt
1/4 teaspoon ground allspice

1/2 teaspoon ground cardamom
1 teaspoon ground ginger
1 to 1 1/4 cups all-purpose flour

Bake the sweet potatoes as for russet potatoes, page 154.

Remove potatoes from oven and allow to cool until you can handle them easily. Peel (the skins should slip off easily), and place flesh in a bowl. Mash with a potato masher or fork; do not puree. There should be just over 1 cup mashed sweet potatoes.

Place the mashed sweet potatoes in the bowl of the pasta machine. Mix about 1 minute.

Turn off machine and sprinkle in salt, allspice, cardamom, ginger, and 1 cup flour. Turn the machine on and mix until the flour is blended with the potatoes, about 1 minute. The dough should be pliable, easy to roll between the palms of your hands, yet sticky if you squeeze it. If it feels too sticky, add additional flour, 2 tablespoons at a time.

Once the dough is mixed, remove it from the machine. Tear off pieces of dough and press them into the extruding portion of your machine. Turn the machine on. As the dough spirals down the corkscrew, turn the machine off and press more dough into the extruder. The gnocchi will start to come out. Sprinkle flour over the surface onto which you are extruding, and have a bowl with flour nearby.

Cut the dough every 1 inch. The gnocchi dough extrudes very quickly, so you will need to work fast. Sprinkle the extruded gnocchi with flour to prevent sticking. Keep the gnocchi in one layer; do not let them pile up as you might with other pasta. They will stick and turn from a pile of gnocchi back into a lump of dough.

When sauce is ready, cook gnocchi in batches, in boiling salted water until they rise to the surface of the water, about 1 to 3 minutes, and then cook 10 to 20 seconds longer. Drain, mix with sauce, and serve immediately.

Sherried Apples and Pecans

YIELD: *4 servings*

2 Granny Smith apples
1/4 cup dry sherry
1/4 cup lightly salted butter

4 teaspoons dark brown sugar
1/4 cup chopped pecans

Peel and core apples, then cut into 1/2 x 1/4-inch pieces. Place in a small bowl and toss with sherry.

Melt butter in a large saucepan over medium heat and cook until bubbly. Add apples and sherry and cook, mixing butter with the sherry. Sprinkle sugar over apples and cook, stirring until sugar dissolves. Bring mixture to a boil and simmer 2 minutes.

Keep warm on low heat while the gnocchi cooks. As soon as each batch of gnocchi is cooked, add to the saucepan and toss gently.

When all the gnocchi are cooked, divide among 4 plates. Sprinkle each serving with 1 tablespoon chopped pecans and serve immediately.

Ricotta Gnocchi with Chunky Tomato Sauce

Ricotta gnocchi are simple, creamy, and delicious. They work well with both whole-milk and part-skim ricotta cheese. Because of the richness of the gnocchi themselves, I prefer ricotta gnocchi with lighter sauces, such as this tomato sauce. The sauce may be prepared up to 3 days in advance and reheated just before serving.

Other recommended accompaniments: Fresh Fennel–Anchovy Sauté (page 65), Herb-Roasted Vegetables (page 49), Puttanesca Sauce (page 139).

Makes 6 servings.

Ricotta Gnocchi

YIELD: *24 ounces*

1 pound ricotta cheese (about
    1 3/4 cups), drained
1 egg, lightly beaten
1/4 cup grated Parmesan cheese
    (1 ounce)

1/4 teaspoon salt
1 1/2 to 2 cups all-purpose flour

Place ricotta in the bowl of the pasta machine. Mix about 1 minute, then add the egg with machine running.

Turn off the machine and sprinkle in Parmesan cheese and salt. Mix until blended, about 1 minute. Turn off the machine and sprinkle in 1 1/2 cups flour. Turn the machine on and run until the flour is incorporated with the ricotta mixture, about 1 minute. Scrape the bowl to incorporate any loose bits. The dough should be pliable, easy to roll between the palms of your hands, yet sticky if you squeeze it. If it feels too sticky, add additional flour, 2 tablespoons at a time.

Once the dough is mixed, remove it from the machine. Tear off pieces of dough and press them into the extruding portion of your machine. Turn the machine on. As the dough spirals down the corkscrew, turn the machine off and press more dough into the extruder. The gnocchi will start to come out. Sprinkle flour over the surface onto which you are extruding, and have a bowl with flour nearby.

Cut the dough every 1 inch. The gnocchi dough extrudes very quickly, so you will need to work fast. Sprinkle the extruded gnocchi with flour to prevent sticking. Keep the gnocchi in one layer; do not let them pile up as you might with other pasta. They will stick and turn from a pile of gnocchi back into a lump of dough.

When sauce is ready, cook gnocchi in batches in boiling salted water until they rise to the surface of the water, about 1 to 3 minutes, and then cook 10 to 20 seconds longer. Drain, mix with sauce, and serve immediately.

Chunky Tomato Sauce

YIELD: *3 cups; 6 servings*

2 tablespoons extra-virgin olive oil
1 medium onion, diced
1 large carrot, peeled and diced
1 stalk celery, diced
1 (28-ounce) can or 1 (26.5-ounce) carton chopped tomatoes

1/2 to 2 teaspoons sugar, or to taste
1/4 teaspoon salt
1/4 teaspoon freshly ground black pepper

Heat olive oil in a large saucepan over medium-high heat. Add onion, carrot, and celery and sauté until onion is translucent and carrot begins to soften, about 20 minutes. Add tomatoes, reduce heat, and simmer 10 minutes.

Taste sauce and if it seems too acidic, add 1/2 teaspoon of sugar. Add additional sugar until the acidity of the sauce is balanced. Add salt and pepper and simmer 2 minutes. Toss with drained gnocchi and serve.

Spinach-Ricotta Gnocchi in Vegetable Soup

This is a simple vegetable soup made hearty and substantial with the addition of these spinach-ricotta gnocchi. They add richness and texture to the broth.

I use pressure cookers often for making such things as stock and broth. I have included instructions here for making the soup both with and without a pressure cooker. The stock can be prepared up to 3 days in advance, or prepared and frozen for up to 2 months. If you are pressed for time, use canned stock. For a really fast meal, use canned vegetable soup mixed with canned stock. The gnocchi will add a homemade touch.

Other recommended accompaniments: Green Bean–Red Onion Sauce (page 55), Roasted Peppers and Herbs (page 141), Tomatoes Fresco (page 67).

Makes 6 to 8 servings.

Spinach-Ricotta Gnocchi

YIELD: *24 ounces*

1 (10-ounce) package frozen chopped spinach
1 cup ricotta cheese
1/2 cup (2 ounces) grated Parmesan cheese

1/8 teaspoon salt
1 large egg, lightly beaten
1 1/2 to 2 cups all-purpose flour

Cook the spinach according to package instructions. Cool slightly, then squeeze all excess moisture from the spinach.

Place ricotta cheese in the bowl of the pasta machine and add spinach, Parmesan cheese, and salt. Mix 1 to 2 minutes, until the ingredients are thoroughly combined, then add the egg with machine running and mix until incorporated.

Turn off the machine and add 1 1/2 cups flour. Turn the machine on and run until the flour is incorporated with the ricotta mixture, about 1 minute. Scrape the bowl to incorporate any loose bits. The dough should be pliable, easy to roll between the palms of your hand, yet sticky if you squeeze it. If it feels too sticky, add additional flour, 2 tablespoons at a time.

Once the dough is mixed, remove it from the machine. Tear off pieces of dough and press them into the extruding portion of your machine. Turn the machine on. As the dough spirals down the corkscrew, turn the machine off and press more dough into the extruder. The gnocchi will start to come out. Sprinkle flour over the surface onto which you are extruding, and have a bowl with flour nearby.

Cut the dough every 1 inch. The gnocchi dough extrudes very quickly, so you will need to work fast. Sprinkle the extruded gnocchi with flour to prevent sticking. Keep the gnocchi in one layer; do not let them pile up as you might with other pasta. They will stick and turn from a pile of gnocchi back into a lump of dough.

When soup is ready, cook gnocchi, in batches, in boiling salted water until they rise to the surface of the water, about 1 to 3 minutes, and then cook 10 to 20 seconds longer. Drain.

Vegetable Soup

YIELD: *9 cups*

VEGETABLE STOCK

2 medium onions, coarsely chopped
4 garlic cloves, peeled and crushed
    slightly
4 medium carrots, cut crosswise into
    2-inch pieces
6 stalks celery, cut crosswise into
    2-inch pieces
2 medium potatoes, scrubbed and
    cut into quarters
10 sprigs parsley
2 bay leaves
8 peppercorns
9 cups water

VEGETABLE SOUP

1 tablespoon extra-virgin olive oil
1 medium onion, thinly sliced
1 carrot, peeled and diced
1 stalk celery, peeled and diced
1 cup frozen whole-kernel corn
8 cups vegetable stock or canned
    vegetable stock or chicken broth
1/2 teaspoon salt
1/4 teaspoon freshly ground pepper
1 recipe Spinach-Ricotta Gnocchi
    (opposite)

Make stock: Place all ingredients in a pressure cooker or stockpot.

For pressure cooker: Cover, securing lid, and bring to high pressure over high heat. Reduce heat to maintain high pressure and cook 12 minutes. Remove from heat, let pressure reduce naturally 10 minutes, then quick-release pressure, following manufacturer's directions.

When the pressure has dropped, remove lid, being careful to keep it turned away from you to avoid the steam.

For standard stockpot: Place all ingredients in a 6- to 8-quart stockpot. Cover and bring to a boil over high heat. Reduce heat and simmer, covered, 45 to 60 minutes.

For either method, let stock cool slightly, then strain, pressing slightly on vegetables to release liquid. Discard vegetables.

Vegetable stock may be refrigerated up to 3 days or frozen up to 2 months. Makes about 2 quarts.

Make soup: Heat olive oil in a stockpot over medium-high heat. Add onion, carrot, and celery and sauté 5 to 8 minutes, until onion is translucent. Add stock and corn and bring to a boil. Reduce heat and simmer 20 minutes, or until carrot is tender. Season with salt and pepper.

To serve, spoon gnocchi into individual serving bowls. Ladle soup into each bowl over gnocchi and serve immediately.

Parsley, Sage, Rosemary & Thyme Ricotta Gnocchi with Creamy Roasted Tomato Sauce

The herb combination here was obviously inspired by the famous (and beautiful) Simon & Garfunkel song. It also happens to taste delicious, especially complimented by the simple, smooth tomato sauce. The sauce takes about 1 hour to prepare, most of it roasting time in the oven. It can be made up to 3 days in advance. Adding a small amount of cream at the end gives the sauce a voluptuous flavor, without feeling heavy and overly rich. This is one of my favorite tomato sauces.

Other recommended accompaniments: Maquechou (page 83), Roasted Red Pepper Sauce (page 25), Vegetable Soup (page 173), Zucchini Mélange (page 57).

Makes 6 servings.

Parsley, Sage, Rosemary & Thyme Ricotta Gnocchi

YIELD: *24 ounces*

1 pound (about 1 3/4 cups) ricotta cheese, drained
1 large egg, lightly beaten
1/4 cup (1 ounce) grated Parmesan cheese
1/4 teaspoon salt
1/4 cup firmly packed chopped fresh parsley

1 1/2 teaspoons minced fresh sage leaves or 1/2 teaspoon dried
1 1/2 teaspoons chopped fresh rosemary leaves or 1/2 teaspoon dried
1 1/2 teaspoons fresh thyme leaves or 1/2 teaspoon dried
1 1/2 to 2 cups all-purpose flour

Place ricotta cheese in the bowl of the pasta machine and mix about 1 minute, then add egg with machine running and mix until incorporated.

Turn off the machine and add Parmesan cheese, salt, parsley, sage, rosemary, and thyme. Turn the machine on and mix until herbs are incorporated into the ricotta mixture, about 1 minute. Turn off the machine and sprinkle in 1 1/2 cups flour. Turn machine on and run until the flour is incorporated into the ricotta mixture, about 1 minute. Scrape the bowl to incorporate any loose bits. The dough should be pliable, easy to roll between the palms of your hands, yet sticky if you squeeze it. If it feels too sticky, add additional flour, 2 tablespoons at a time.

Once the dough is mixed, remove it from the machine. Tear off pieces of dough and press them into the extruding portion of your machine. Turn the machine on. As the dough spirals down the corkscrew, turn the machine off and press more dough into the extruder. The gnocchi will start to come out. Sprinkle flour over the surface onto which you are extruding, and have a bowl with flour nearby.

Cut the dough every 1 inch. The gnocchi dough extrudes very quickly, so you will need to work fast. Sprinkle the extruded gnocchi with flour to prevent sticking. Keep the gnocchi in one layer; do not let them pile up as you might with other pasta. They will tend to stick and turn from a pile of gnocchi back into a lump of dough.

When sauce is ready, cook gnocchi in batches in boiling salted water until they rise to the surface of the water, about 1 to 3 minutes, and then cook 10 to 20 seconds longer. Drain.

Creamy Roasted Tomato Sauce

YIELD: *2 1/4 cups; 6 servings*

2 tablespoons extra-virgin olive oil
1 large red onion, ends trimmed,
    outer layer of skin removed,
    and cut in half crosswise
6 cloves garlic, peeled, ends
    trimmed, and cut in half
1 (28-ounce) can or 1 (26.5-ounce)
    carton chopped tomatoes,
    drained

2 tablespoons white wine
1 teaspoon salt
1/4 teaspoon freshly ground black
    pepper
1 to 2 teaspoons sugar, or to taste
1/4 cup whipping cream

Preheat oven to 425F (220C). Spoon olive oil into a 13 x 9-inch baking pan and tilt pan to coat bottom with oil. Place onion halves, cut side down, in olive oil. Scatter garlic cloves around the pan. Pour in chopped tomatoes. Drizzle with wine.

Bake 30 minutes, until onion and garlic are soft when pierced with a knife. Remove the onion. The outer layer or two may still be tough or firm; remove and discard. Chop remaining onion coarsely and return onion to the tomatoes.

Bake 15 minutes. Remove from oven; much of the watery liquid will have evaporated. Process mixture in a food processor or blender until pureed. Pour the mixture through a strainer to remove any skin or seeds for a delicately smooth sauce. (Sauce may be prepared in advance up to this point. Refrigerate for up to 3 days.)

Pour tomato sauce into a small saucepan and heat over medium-high heat. Season with salt, pepper, and sugar. Stir in cream. Bring to a boil, then immediately reduce heat and simmer 1 minute. To serve, place cooked gnocchi on individual plates and spoon sauce over each serving. Pass extra sauce in a bowl.

Not Just Pasta

Pasta machines are designed primarily for making pasta, obviously. But they also can be used to make other doughs, such as breadsticks, crackers, and cookies, with pleasing results. The procedure for making these products is somewhat different from that for pasta making, and this chapter explains the necessary techniques. The pasta machine is especially useful for cookie batter that you ordinarily would roll into logs by hand or would force through a cookie press. The whole procedure is cleaner and much easier.

Most pasta machines come with a breadstick die, which can be used for most of the recipes in this chapter (others call for the lasagne die). There are machines that also come with various cookie dies, and it is fun to experiment with them.

Rosemary-Pepper Breadsticks

The pasta machine is particularly great for breadsticks, which can be tedious to make when you have to roll out each individual breadstick by hand. These breadsticks are long, thin, and crunchy, plus they're extremely low in fat. Most machines come with a breadstick die. For some machines, the macaroni or penne die comes in two parts. I recommend using this die without the inner attachment. This way you can make several breadsticks at a time, instead of just one.

YIELD: *36 breadsticks*

4 cups all-purpose flour
1 teaspoon sugar
1 1/4 teaspoons salt
1 tablespoon minced fresh rosemary
  or 1 teaspoon dried
1/4 teaspoon freshly ground black
  pepper

1 package (about 2 1/2 teaspoons)
  active dry yeast
1 1/2 teaspoons olive oil
About 1 cup lukewarm water
  (110F, 45C)
Kosher salt, for sprinkling

Combine flour, sugar, salt, rosemary, pepper, and yeast in pasta machine and mix 1 minute to combine.

Mix olive oil and 1 cup water in a measuring cup.

With pasta machine running, slowly add water mixture and mix until dough forms a ball. If it seems too dry, add more water, 1 tablespoon at a time. If it seems too wet, add more flour, 1 tablespoon at a time. The dough should not feel sticky when you squeeze it in your hand, but it should not be too dry either.

When a ball has formed, mix 3 minutes to knead dough. Remove dough from pasta machine. Form dough into a ball and place in a lightly oiled bowl. Turn dough to coat with oil. Cover with a cloth, set in a warm, draft-free place, and let rise until doubled in bulk, about 1 hour.

Preheat oven to 425F (220C). Line a baking sheet with parchment paper or spray with baking spray.

Punch down dough and prepare to extrude. The procedure for extruding breadsticks is slightly different from that for pasta. Because of the nature of yeast dough, if you have the entire ball of dough in the machine, the ball will keep picking up the dough as it tries to go into the extruder, and nothing will extrude. Instead, keep the bulk of the dough outside the machine and tear off pieces of dough and press them into the extruding portion of your machine. Turn the machine on. As the dough spirals down the corkscrew, turn the machine off and press more dough into the extruder. The breadsticks will start to come out.

Cut the breadsticks at 10- to 12-inch lengths. Place on baking sheet 1/2 inch apart. Brush the breadsticks lightly with water and sprinkle with kosher salt.

Bake 25 minutes or until pale gold for slightly chewy, yet crunchy breadsticks. For very crisp breadsticks, bake 10 minutes more or until golden brown.

Cool breadsticks on wire racks and store in a plastic container.

Pretzels

You can't beat the taste of pretzels fresh from the oven, and with the pasta machine they are easy to make. I recommend using the breadstick die, as the machine can be extruding while you are shaping a pretzel. Because the breadstick die is narrow, this recipe works best for smaller soft pretzels, about 3 to 4 inches across when baked. Larger pretzels have a tendency to break during preparation.

Cooking the pretzels is a two-step procedure. The pretzels are first dipped in a simmering water–baking soda bath, then baked at a high temperature. The baking soda helps make the pretzels brown and shiny; without it, the pretzels will remain pale and dry looking. It takes a little practice to get the hang of dipping the uncooked pretzels, but once you try it a few times, it will be easy.

You could omit the baking-soda bath and brush the pretzels with an egg beaten with 1 tablespoon water. This will give the pretzels a different flavor, but they will still look and taste great.

YIELD: *about 32 (3-inch) pretzels*

4 cups all-purpose flour
1 tablespoon sugar
1 teaspoon salt
1 package (about 2 1/2 teaspoons)
    active dry yeast
1 tablespoon vegetable oil
1 cup plus 2 tablespoons lukewarm
    water (110F, 45C)

4 quarts water
1/4 cup baking soda
Kosher salt, for sprinkling
Optional toppings: sesame seeds,
    poppy seeds, garlic salt, onion
    flakes
Mustard, for dipping

Combine flour, sugar, salt, and yeast in pasta machine and mix to combine for 1 minute.

Mix oil and water in a 2-cup measuring cup.

With pasta machine running, slowly add water mixture and mix until dough forms a ball. If it seems too dry, add more water, 1 tablespoon at a time. If it seems too wet, add more flour, 1 tablespoon at a time. The dough should not feel sticky when you squeeze it in your hand, but it should not be overly dry.

When a ball has formed, mix 3 minutes to knead dough. Remove dough from pasta machine. Form dough into a ball and place in a lightly oiled bowl. Turn dough to coat with oil. Cover with a cloth, set in a warm, draft-free place, and let rise until doubled in bulk, about 1 hour.

Preheat oven to 425F (220C). Line a baking sheet with parchment paper or spray with baking spray. Pour 4 quarts of water into large pot and bring to a boil.

Punch down dough and prepare to extrude. The procedure for extruding pretzels is slightly different from that for pasta. Because of the nature of yeast dough, if you have the entire ball of dough in the machine, the ball will keep picking up the dough as it tries to go into the extruder, and nothing will extrude. Instead, keep the bulk of the dough outside the machine and tear off pieces of dough and press them into the extruding portion of your machine. Turn the machine on. As the dough spirals down the corkscrew, turn the machine off and press more dough into the extruder. The dough will start to come out.

Cut dough at 10- to 12-inch lengths. Form each length into a pretzel shape, pinching the ends to join them. As you form each pretzel, place on baking sheet 1 inch apart. Let rest 10 to 15 minutes.

When the water comes to a boil, add baking soda and reduce to a simmer. Using a slotted spatula, place a pretzel in the water and cook about 40 seconds. Remove with a spatula, being careful to maintain the pretzel shape. (Pretzels that are much larger than the spatula have a tendency to break.) Drain off excess water, then return pretzel to baking sheet, placing about 1 inch apart. Sprinkle pretzels with salt or one of the optional toppings.

Bake 15 to 20 minutes or until golden brown for soft pretzels. For crunchier pretzels, bake 5 minutes more, and store uncovered overnight.

Pretzels are best if eaten within a day. The pretzels will be soft when they come out of the oven and will remain soft for several hours. Stored overnight, pretzels will begin to become hard and slightly chewy. To store the pretzels and retain their soft texture, freeze in an airtight container and reheat in a toaster oven.

Seeded Cheddar Straws

These Cheddar cracker sticks are always a hit at parties, and are quick to make in a pasta machine. A variety of seeds, plus a touch of cornmeal, give these cheese straws an appealing crunch. Use either the breadstick die or the macaroni or penne die without the inner insert. With the macaroni or penne die, you can make several straws at a time, instead of just one.

YIELD: *about 72 (3-inch) Cheddar straws*

3/4 cup all-purpose flour
1/8 teaspoon salt
2 tablespoons cornmeal
1 tablespoon toasted sesame seeds
     (see Note, opposite)
1 tablespoon poppy seeds
1 teaspoon caraway seeds

8 ounces Cheddar cheese, grated
     (about 2 cups), at room
     temperature
5 to 6 tablespoons unsalted butter,
     cut into small pieces, room
     temperature

Preheat oven to 400F (205C). Combine flour, salt, cornmeal, sesame seeds, poppy seeds, and caraway seeds in pasta machine bowl. Mix 1 minute, until well combined. Add cheese and mix 1 minute.

Add 5 tablespoons of the butter and mix 3 to 5 minutes, until mixture is blended. The dough should hold together. If it is still crumbly, add the remaining 1 tablespoon butter.

Extrude, using the breadstick die, or the penne or macaroni die without the inner attachment (if your machine will work this way). Let dough extrude about 3 inches, cut, and place straws 1 inch apart on ungreased baking sheets; cheese straws will spread and flatten slightly.

Bake 10 to 15 minutes or until edges are golden brown. Cool 1 minute on baking sheets, then remove to wire racks to cool completely.

Store in an airtight container, refrigerated, up to 1 week, or in the freezer up to 3 months.

Note To toast sesame seeds on the stovetop, place sesame seeds in a small, dry, heavy-bottomed skillet over medium-high heat, stirring frequently. When seeds begin to turn golden brown, about 2 to 3 minutes, remove from pan and let cool.

To toast sesame seeds in the microwave, place sesame seeds on a microwave-safe plate and microwave on HIGH 4 minutes. Stir and check; seeds should begin to turn golden. Microwave on HIGH 1 minute and check again. Continue cooking on HIGH in 1-minute intervals until the seeds turn golden brown. Set aside and let cool.

Chocolate Crisps

This recipe produces a crisp, tasty cookie that is very low in fat; the only fat it contains comes from the egg. The cookies are thin, crunchy, and chocolatey.

The lasagne die produces the best-textured cookie and is the easiest to use. Other dies make interesting shapes. It is fun to use a ziti or penne die, because of the distinctive pasta shape; the cookies actually look like pasta. However, this is more challenging to work with, because the dough tends to close up at the end as you cut it. Cut the ziti at a 1-inch length and turn off the machine as you place it on the cookie sheet. The ziti cookies need to cook 3 to 4 minutes longer.

Fettuccine and papardelle also make good shapes, but the fettuccine in particular is very delicate. If you have the time, twist each strand for a decorative cookie.

YIELD: *about 60 (1 1/2-inch) squares*

1/2 cup all-purpose flour	1/8 teaspoon salt
1/2 cup semolina flour	1 large egg
2 tablespoons unsweetened cocoa powder	1/2 teaspoon vanilla extract
6 tablespoons sugar	Water, if needed

Preheat oven to 350F (175C). Line 2 baking sheets with parchment paper or lightly grease. Set aside.

Combine flours, cocoa, sugar, and salt in pasta machine bowl. Mix 1 minute, until blended.

Lightly beat together egg and vanilla.

With the pasta machine running, slowly add egg mixture to the flour over a period of 3 minutes. Let machine continue to mix another minute. The dough should consist of lumps the size of peas and walnut halves. If it seems too dry, gradually add water, 1/2 tablespoon at a time. If it seems too wet, add more flour, 1 tablespoon at a time.

When the dough is the proper consistency, extrude according to the manufacturer's instructions. This dough is delicate and heats up quickly, so I recommend making it in smaller batches. As the dough goes through the extruder, it may eventually come together in a solid mass. If this happens, stop the machine every few minutes and push small clumps of dough into the extruding area, as in the preparation of breadsticks (pages 180–181).

Using lasagne die, let dough extrude about 6 inches, then cut and stop machine. Cut dough into 1 1/2-inch squares and place on prepared baking sheets about 1/2 inch apart.

Bake 10 to 11 minutes or until firm. Remove and cool on wire rack. Store cookies in an airtight container for several days, or freeze up to 3 months.

Variation

Place 3 ounces (1/2 cup) semisweet chocolate chips in a microwave-safe bowl and microwave on HIGH 45 seconds; stir. If there are still unmelted bits, microwave 20 seconds and stir until melted. Using a spoon, scoop up some of the chocolate, then drizzle chocolate over cookies. Let cool until set.

Ginger Thins

These ginger thins are beautifully crisp and delicate, and as addictive as potato chips. I recommend using the lasagne die for these cookies; they work best as a thin cookie, rather than the thicker cookies produced with the breadstick die.

Mixing the batter for these cookies takes slightly longer than it does when using a conventional electric mixer, but the results are worth it. The cookies come out extra thin. You could never roll them this thin using a rolling pin, without using so much flour that the cookies would become tough and hard. It may seem like a lot of cookies, but they will disappear as quickly as you make them. They also freeze well.

YIELD: *about 200 (1 1/2-inch) cookies*

2 1/2 to 3 cups all-purpose flour	1 tablespoon ground ginger
1/2 cup granulated sugar	1/2 cup unsalted butter, cut into
1/2 cup packed brown sugar	8 pieces and softened
1/4 teaspoon salt	1 large egg
2 teaspoons baking soda	1 teaspoon vanilla extract
1/2 teaspoon ground allspice	1/4 cup molasses

Preheat oven to 350F (175C). Line 2 baking sheets with parchment paper or lightly grease.

Combine 2 1/2 cups of the flour, granulated sugar, brown sugar, salt, baking soda, allspice, and ginger in pasta machine bowl. Mix 3 to 5 minutes, until thoroughly blended, using a spoon to break apart brown sugar, if needed. Add butter and mix 3 to 5 minutes or until mixture is the texture of cornmeal.

Whisk egg slightly in a measuring cup. Whisk in vanilla and molasses until blended. With pasta machine running, slowly add egg mixture to flour mixture. Let the machine continue to mix another minute, scraping the sides occasionally as the mixtures come together. The dough will be slightly sticky at this point. Add remaining 1/2 cup flour and stir until thoroughly incorporated. The dough should not be sticky; pinch off a piece and roll it between your fingers. If it sticks, add a little more flour. If the dough is moldable but not sticky, it's the correct consistency.

Extrude, using the lasagne die. The dough comes out quickly and is delicate; turn the machine off for each cookie. Let dough extrude 1 1/2 inches, turn off machine, and cut. Place squares close together on prepared baking sheets; dough does not spread very much during baking. If desired, take scraps of dough and roll them into tiny dots and squiggles and decorate the squares with these designs.

Bake cookies 6 minutes or until firm and very pale gold around the edges. Cool on baking sheets 1 minute, then remove to wire racks to cool completely.

Store in airtight containers up to 1 week, or freeze up to 3 months.

Coconut Batons

These shortbread-style cookies work very well in the pasta machine. Use the breadstick die, or the penne die with the insert removed. I prefer the breadstick die because the dough comes out fairly quickly, and it is easier to work with dough coming out of just one hole. These are delicious, buttery cookies, highlighted by toasted coconut. For an extravagant treat, dip the ends in chocolate.

YIELD: *about 96 (1 1/2-inch) cookies*

1 cup shredded coconut
1 cup all-purpose flour
1/3 cup powdered sugar

1/4 teaspoon salt
1/2 cup unsalted butter, cut into
    small pieces and softened

Preheat oven to 350F (175C). Toast coconut: Spread coconut on a baking sheet and bake 2 minutes. Stir and check. Bake another 2 to 3 minutes, stir, and check. It should start to smell toasted. When coconut begins to turn golden brown, remove from oven immediately and stir. It will continue to toast slowly as it cools.

Combine flour, powdered sugar, and salt in pasta machine bowl. Add cooled coconut and mix 3 to 5 minutes, until thoroughly blended.

Add butter and mix 3 to 5 minutes or until mixture is blended. The dough should just come together, but not be crumbly.

Extrude, using the breadstick die. Let dough extrude 1 1/2 inches and cut. Place batons 1/2 inch apart on ungreased baking sheets; dough does not spread very much during baking.

Bake cookies 15 to 18 minutes or until firm and pale gold. Cool on baking sheets 1 minute, then remove to wire racks and cool completely.

Store in airtight containers up to 1 week, or freeze up to 2 months.

Variation

Place 1/2 cup semisweet chocolate chips in a microwave-safe bowl and microwave on HIGH 45 seconds; stir. If there are still unmelted bits, microwave 20 seconds and stir until melted. Dip ends of cookies in melted chocolate, then dip in a bowl with a small amount of shredded coconut. Place on a foil-lined baking sheet to set for several hours. Store chocolate-dipped cookies in refrigerator or freezer.

Cornmeal Crunchies

Cornmeal lends an appealing crunch to cookies, and rosemary gives these an interesting flavor. I love the unexpected combination, but if it sounds unappealing to you, by all means omit it, or feel free to substitute other herbs or spices. This recipe is adapted from the Rosemary Zaletti recipe I contributed to The Joy of Coffee *by Corby Kummer (Chapters, 1995).*

Some pasta machines come with a cookie die, which yields cookies about 1/8 inch thick and 1/2 to 1 inch wide. I tried this recipe using both the cookie die and the breadstick die. The cookie die yields a thin, crisp cookie, while the breadstick die yields a thicker, crunchy cookie. Both are addictively delicious. The yield refers to cookies made using the breadstick die.

YIELD: *about 72 cookies*

1 cup yellow cornmeal
1 1/3 cups all-purpose flour
3/4 cup sugar
1/4 teaspoon salt
3/4 teaspoon dried rosemary

1/2 cup unsalted butter, cut into
   small pieces and softened
1 large egg
1 1/2 teaspoons vanilla extract

Preheat oven to 375F (190C). Line 2 baking sheets with parchment paper or lightly grease.

Combine cornmeal, flour, sugar, salt, and rosemary in pasta machine bowl. Mix 3 to 5 minutes or until thoroughly blended.

Add butter and mix 3 to 5 minutes or until mixture is combined. The dough should be the consistency of coarse cornmeal and come together slightly.

Whisk egg lightly in a measuring cup. Whisk in vanilla. With the pasta machine running, slowly add egg mixture to the flour. Let the machine continue to mix another minute, scraping the sides occasionally as the mixtures come together. The dough should not be sticky; pinch off a piece and roll it between your fingers. If it sticks, add a little more flour. If the dough is moldable but not sticky, it's the right consistency.

Extrude, using the breadstick die. Let dough extrude 4 to 5 inches and cut. Cut 6 or 7 strands, then turn off machine to shape cookies. Shape each strand into an O-shape, joining the ends. Place on prepared baking sheets about 1/2 inch apart.

Bake cookies 12 to 15 minutes or until firm and pale gold around the edges. Cool on baking sheets 1 minute, then remove to wire racks to cool completely.

Store in airtight containers up to 1 week, or freeze up to 3 months.

Almond Pretzel Cookies

This recipe was inspired by a sour cream cookie in The Joy of Cooking *(MacMillan, 1975). I love the flavor of almonds, and adapted the recipe. Molded cookies such as these work well in a pasta machine, and the dough does not need to chill.*

Crystallized sugar, available in the baking section of the supermarket with the cake-decorating supplies, makes these cookies look that much more festive.

YIELD: *about 5 dozen cookies*

1/4 cup whole almonds
1 cup sugar
3 cups all-purpose flour
1/2 teaspoon salt
1 teaspoon baking powder
1 cup unsalted butter, cut into small
    pieces and softened

1 egg
1/4 cup sour cream
1/2 teaspoon almond extract
1 egg white, lightly beaten
Crystallized sugar

Preheat oven to 375F (190C). Lightly grease 2 baking sheets and set aside.

Toast almonds: Spread almonds on an ungreased baking sheet or small pan and bake 5 to 10 minutes, checking frequently, until almonds smell toasted. To test, cut an almond in half. It should be pale brown at the center. Remove from oven immediately and set aside until cooled.

Combine almonds and 1/4 cup of the sugar in the bowl of a food processor. Process until almonds are finely ground. Be careful not to overprocess and turn the mixture into almond butter.

Combine flour, remaining 3/4 cup sugar, salt, and baking powder in pasta machine bowl. Add ground almond mixture. Mix 3 to 5 minutes or until well combined.

Add butter and mix 3 to 5 minutes or until mixture is crumbly.

Whisk egg in a measuring cup and whisk in sour cream and almond extract. With machine running, slowly add egg mixture. Mix another minute. The dough should come together and be moist but not sticky.

Extrude, using the breadstick die. Let dough extrude about 6 inches, cut, and turn off machine (the dough comes out very quickly). The dough can be delicate, so be gentle. Hold each end and bring them toward each other. Twist the ends around each other and join at the center, forming a pretzel shape. Place about 1 inch apart on prepared baking sheets. Brush cookies with egg white and sprinkle with crystallized sugar.

Bake cookies 12 to 15 minutes or until set and very pale gold. Cool on baking sheets 1 minute, then remove to wire racks to cool completely.

Store in airtight containers up to 1 week, or freeze up to 2 months.

Citrus Delights

I love citrus flavors, especially lemon. Lemon is the dominant flavor in these cookies, which are flecked with lime zest and orange zest. The lemon glaze gives them a wonderful tang. You can make these cookies with the breadstick die, but I prefer to make them with a cookie die; they are more delicate.

YIELD: *about 10 dozen cookies*

2 1/4 cups all-purpose flour
1 cup sugar
1/4 teaspoon salt
1/2 teaspoon baking soda
Grated zest of 1 lime
Grated zest of 1 orange
1/2 cup unsalted butter, cut into small
    pieces and softened

1 large egg
2 teaspoons lemon extract
2 tablespoons fresh lemon juice

GLAZE
1/4 cup fresh lemon juice
1/4 cup sugar

Preheat oven to 375F (190C). Line 2 baking sheets with parchment paper or lightly grease.

Combine flour, sugar, salt, and baking soda in pasta machine bowl. Mix 1 minute or until combined. Add lime and orange zest and mix 1 minute.

Add butter and mix 3 to 5 minutes or until the mixture is crumbly.

Whisk egg in a measuring cup and whisk in lemon extract and lemon juice. With machine running, add egg mixture. Let the machine continue to mix another minute. The dough should come together and be moist but not sticky. If it is too sticky, add more flour, 1 tablespoon at a time.

Extrude, using the cookie die or breadstick die. Let dough extrude 2 to 3 inches, cut, and place on prepared baking sheets. Dough comes out quickly, so turn machine off and on for each cookie, if needed. Place cookies about 1/2 inch apart on prepared baking sheets; dough does not spread very much during baking.

Bake cookies 12 to 14 minutes or until edges begin to turn golden brown.

While cookies are baking, prepare glaze: Combine lemon juice and sugar in a small saucepan. Bring to a boil over high heat, stirring frequently, until sugar dissolves. Reduce heat and simmer 2 minutes. Remove from heat.

Leave cookies on baking sheet and immediately brush with the glaze. Serve immediately, or allow to remain on baking sheets several hours.

Store in an airtight container 4 to 5 days, or up to 3 months in the freezer. Cookies will stick slightly, but will separate easily.

Sources

Bouchard Family Farm
RR#1 Box 690
Fort Kent, ME 04743
(800) 239-3237 or (207) 834-3237

Bouchard sells a wonderful silverskin buckwheat flour, made from plants that grow only in northern Maine.

Eastern Lamejun
145 Belmont St.
Belmont, MA 02178
(617) 484-5239

Specializing in Middle Eastern and Armenian goods, Eastern Lamejun carries nearly 100 spices and herbs.

Fiddler's Green Farm
P.O. Box 254
Belfast, ME 04915
(800) 729-7935 or (207) 338-3872

On a weekly basis, Fiddler's Green grinds a variety of organic flours, including whole wheat, cornmeal, and rye flour.

The Great Valley Mills
1774 County Line Rd.
Barto, PA 19504
(800) 688-6455

This food catalog includes a variety of flours, including some of the best whole-wheat flour I've tasted.

Indian Foods & Spices
80 River St.
Cambridge, MA 02139
(617) 497-6144

Specializing in hard-to-find Indian items, this company sells dozens of spices, both whole and ground.

King Arthur Flour
The Baker's Catalog
PO Box 876
Norwich, VT 05055-0876
(800) 827-6836

King Arthur makes my favorite all-purpose flour, which is available in supermarkets in New England. They also sell it by mail, along with a wide choice of other flours, from millet and chestnut to durum and semolina. They also sell various pasta-making accessories.

Vitantonia
6225 Cochran Rd.
Solon, OH 44139
(800) 732-4444

Vitantonia carries an extensive selection of pasta-making accessories, including both Imperia and Atlas pasta rollers, as well as ravioli stamps and drying racks.

Metric Conversion Charts

Comparison to Metric Measure

When You Know	Symbol	Multiply By	To Find	Symbol
teaspoons	tsp	5.0	milliliters	ml
tablespoons	tbsp	15.0	milliliters	ml
fluid ounces	fl. oz.	30.0	milliliters	ml
cups	c	0.24	liters	l
pints	pt.	0.47	liters	l
quarts	qt.	0.95	liters	l
ounces	oz.	28.0	grams	g
pounds	lb.	0.45	kilograms	kg
Fahrenheit	F	5/9 (after subtracting 32)	Celsius	C

Fahrenheit to Celsius

F	C
200–205	95
220–225	105
245–250	120
275	135
300–305	150
325–330	165
345–350	175
370–375	190
400–405	205
425–430	220
445–450	230
470–475	245
500	260

Liquid Measure to Milliliters

1/4 teaspoon	=	1.25 milliliters
1/2 teaspoon	=	2.5 milliliters
3/4 teaspoon	=	3.75 milliliters
1 teaspoon	=	5.0 milliliters
1 1/4 teaspoons	=	6.25 milliliters
1 1/2 teaspoons	=	7.5 milliliters
1 3/4 teaspoons	=	8.75 milliliters
2 teaspoons	=	10.0 milliliters
1 tablespoon	=	15.0 milliliters
2 tablespoons	=	30.0 milliliters

Liquid Measure to Liters

1/4 cup	=	0.06 liters
1/2 cup	=	0.12 liters
3/4 cup	=	0.18 liters
1 cup	=	0.24 liters
1 1/4 cups	=	0.30 liters
1 1/2 cups	=	0.36 liters
2 cups	=	0.48 liters
2 1/2 cups	=	0.60 liters
3 cups	=	0.72 liters
3 1/2 cups	=	0.84 liters
4 cups	=	0.96 liters
4 1/2 cups	=	1.08 liters
5 cups	=	1.20 liters
5 1/2 cups	=	1.32 liters

Index